"Chris Durso is a young pastor with an authority beyond his years. His edgy demeanor gives him license to speak life and truth into people who are lost and broken. Even seasoned Christians will rediscover their first love through his passionate words. His revelation of grace and the truth of the gospel will compel and inspire you to step into your God-given purpose and destiny."

—BRIAN HOUSTON, global senior pastor, Hillsong Church

"*The Heist* is a story of grace and restoration. Readers will find refuge in the promise that God's grace can and will stop shame in its tracks."

—CHRISTINE CAINE, cofounder of the A21Campaign and
Propel Women

"Gutsy. Unexpected. Refreshing. Chris Durso explains the story of saving Grace in a language that both the world and the Church, sinners and so-called saints, can understand. *The Heist* walks us down the road with the prodigal son, inviting us to come home to the One who has a grace-party waiting. Fresh and accessible, I believe this book will help many live fully and freely in Jesus."

—LOUIE GIGLIO, pastor of Passion City Church, founder of Passion
Conferences, author of *Goliath Must Fall*

"I have the privilege of being Chris Durso's friend, and I have watched him teach that Jesus is the way to real life. I believe *The Heist* has the potential to remind people that whatever has been stolen or destroyed can be redeemed in an *instant*. I love this book and I highly recommend its author!"

—CARL LENTZ, lead pastor, Hillsong New York

"*The Heist* is packed with hard-hitting, attention-grabbing, and life-altering truth. Chris Durso masterfully portrays the death and resurrection of Jesus in a new and unprecedented way, that will not only catch readers off guard but draw them closer to Jesus."

—CRAIG GROESCHEL, founder and senior pastor of Life.Church and
New York Times best-selling author

"Chris Durso manages to beautifully remind us that just like the prodigal son, we are all able to return home into the loving arms of our God."

—JUDAH SMITH, lead pastor of the City Church, Seattle

"Most of our lives are spent avoiding anything that resembles a robbery. However, Pastor Chris Durso has cleverly used a metaphorical illustration to exemplify the powerful, stealthy work of grace. This grace removes the plagues from our hall of shame, enabling the guilty to appear faultless before God's throne. To the wounded, read this powerful book with the doors unlocked and the alarm off, anticipating the possibility of a new life! This is *The Heist* for which the human soul longs!"

—T. D. JAKES SR., senior pastor, The Potter's House of Dallas

"I'm so glad Chris Durso took the time to pen *The Heist*. It will change how you view Jesus and his death on the Cross. It will reveal how the road to salvation is anything but a 'boring, old Bible story' and portray Jesus as the Mastermind working to rescue us from the clutches of Satan."

—LISA BEVERE, minister and *New York Times* best-selling author of *Without Rival*

"*The Heist* isn't just a book that creatively retells the story of Jesus dying on the cross. It's a book with a timeless, vitally important message that we are all loved by God, and that it doesn't matter what we do or where we are; we can always run into his arms."

—JENTEZEN FRANKLIN, *New York Times* best-selling author and pastor of Free Chapel Worship Center

"Pastor Chris has a unique ability to help us see something familiar through a different lens. This book is an incredible picture of how God came in to our spiritual homes and robbed everything that was never meant to live there. When we receive the revelation of this kind of grace, we can't help but step up and live from a free and secure place. This book is a necessary read for each of us because we all need the fullness of this grace revelation."

—ALEX SEELEY, author and pastor, The Belonging Co., Nashville

"In a culture that is constantly drowning under the strong currents of condemnation and shame, Pastor Chris Durso has thrown us all a timely lifeline with his powerful new book *The Heist*."

—PASTOR ROBERT MADU

"My son Chris Durso is not just a brilliant writer. Rather, his ability to take a doctrine of the faith and put it into everyday language is simply masterful! Jesus taught the people "as they could understand." This is the Gospel: how heaven robbed hell. This is the heart of God! What a concept!"

—MICHAEL DURSO, senior pastor, Christ Tabernacle

It is by Grace!

THE HEIST

ALSO BY CHRIS DURSO

Misfit

THE HEIST

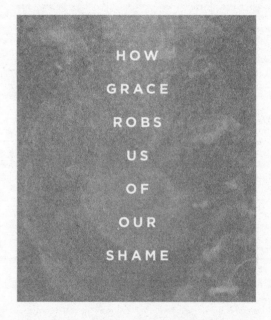

HOW

GRACE

ROBS

US

OF

OUR

SHAME

CHRIS DURSO

WATERBROOK

The Heist

All Scripture quotations, unless otherwise indicated, are taken from the Holy Bible, New International Version®, NIV®. Copyright © 1973, 1978, 1984, 2011 by Biblica Inc.® Used by permission. All rights reserved worldwide. Scripture quotations marked (AMPC) are taken from the Amplified Bible Classic Edition. Copyright © 1954, 1958, 1962, 1964, 1965, 1987 by the Lockman Foundation. Used by permission. (www.Lockman.org). Scripture quotations marked (ERV) are taken from the Holy Bible: Easy-to-Read Version © 2006 by Bible League International. Used by permission. Scripture quotations marked (ESV) are taken from the ESV® Bible (the Holy Bible, English Standard Version®), copyright © 2001 by Crossway, a publishing ministry of Good News Publishers. Used by permission. All rights reserved. Scripture quotations marked (KJV) are taken from the King James Version. Scripture quotations marked (MSG) are taken from The Message. Copyright © by Eugene H. Peterson 1993, 1994, 1995, 1996, 2000, 2001, 2002. Used by permission of Tyndale House Publishers Inc. Scripture quotations marked (NASB) are taken from the New American Standard Bible®. Copyright © 1960, 1962, 1963, 1968, 1971, 1972, 1973, 1975, 1977, 1995 by the Lockman Foundation. Used by permission. (www.Lockman.org). Scripture quotations marked (NKJV) are taken from the New King James Version®. Copyright © 1982 by Thomas Nelson Inc. Used by permission. All rights reserved. Scripture quotations marked (NLV) are taken from the Holy Bible, New Life Version. Copyright 1969, 1976, 1978, 1983, 1986, 1992, 1997, 2003, Christian Literature International, P. O. Box 777, Canby, OR 97013. Used by permission. Scripture quotations marked (NLT) are taken from the Holy Bible, New Living Translation, copyright © 1996, 2004, 2007, 2013, 2015 by Tyndale House Foundation. Used by permission of Tyndale House Publishers Inc., Carol Stream, Illinois 60188. All rights reserved. Scripture quotations marked (NRSV) are taken from the New Revised Standard Version Bible, copyright © 1989, Division of Christian Education of the National Council of the Churches of Christ in the United States of America. Used by permission. All rights reserved.

Italics in Scripture quotations reflect the author's added emphasis, except where italics are found in the original.

Trade Paperback ISBN 978-1-60142-866-0
eBook ISBN 978-1-60142-867-7

Copyright © 2017 by Chris Durso

Cover design and cover image by Hannah Burton

Published in the United States by WaterBrook, an imprint of the Crown Publishing Group, a division of Penguin Random House LLC, New York.

WATERBROOK® and its deer colophon are registered trademarks of Penguin Random House LLC.

The Cataloging-in-Publication Data is on file with the Library of Congress.

Printed in the United States of America
2017—First Edition

10 9 8 7 6 5 4 3 2 1

SPECIAL SALES
Most WaterBrook books are available at special quantity discounts when purchased in bulk by corporations, organizations, and special-interest groups. Custom imprinting or excerpting can also be done to fit special needs. For information, please e-mail specialmarketscms@penguinrandomhouse.com or call 1-800-603-7051.

—

I dedicate this book to my precious wife, Yahris Durso. Thank you for giving me the best parts of you, accepting me just as I am, and doing all that you can to support the high calling on our lives as parents, pastors, and leaders. Your life and your love are the greatest evidence of God's grace in my life.

CONTENTS

FOREWORD

One of my earliest memories is from when I was living in Queens, New York, as a kid. My brother and I were walking down an alley, and we were mugged by kids just a bit older than us. Their weapon of choice was a clothes hanger that they thrust through my brother's nose. After they ran off, I remember my brother trying to use dirt from the street to stop the bleeding.

I share this memory with you to emphasize one main point: *you have to be tough to make it in Queens!*

This is one of the many reasons I love Chris Durso—he is 100 percent pure Queens. New Yorkers already have a reputation for resilience and drive that the rest of the world admires. When you add the character of Queens, you combine grit and street smarts to that formula.

That's who Chris Durso is at his core.

Street-smart, gritty, driven, and resilient, he is the perfect person to write a book called *The Heist*.

He has a unique way of communicating the message of Jesus

to a world that is put off by a faith that feels too sanitized and safe.

While I love the subtitle, *How Grace Robs Us of Our Shame,* I still prefer the subtitle Chris and I pitched to the publishers when I first heard of this project. In the early stages of this book, Chris shared with me his idea for a working title: *The Heist: The One Crime Jesus Did Commit!*

I don't think we are quite ready to see Jesus as the thief who died between two thieves.

I understand that we feel more comfortable saying "grace stole our shame," but it was Jesus who cracked the safe to the human heart and replaced despair with hope.

It was Jesus who, through His death and resurrection, robbed the grave of its power. And it was Jesus who descended into and endured the depths in order to set the captives free.

"Grace" is just a fancy way to describe the greatest heist in history.

Somewhere in between these two statements of grace and thievery is the power of *The Heist.*

Chris Durso is both a man of the Word and a man of the world. He has deep and powerful faith that is shaped by the Scriptures, yet he maintains the ability to speak to the hearts and minds of people who don't know Jesus.

Chris has taken on the challenge of becoming a translator of the gospel for a generation that speaks a unique language. His life mission is to bring the message of Jesus to this world in an honest, gritty, street-smart way.

On a personal level, our stories came together long before I was aware of it, and they have been interwoven ever since. I had no idea I was a part of his story, but when I met Chris's beautiful wife, Yahris, the first thing she said to me was, "You are the reason Chris is a pastor and in ministry today."

Apparently Chris happened to be at an event where I was speaking years ago. He was far from God and running in the opposite direction. It was during that talk that God took hold of him, and Chris returned to the calling he knew was upon his life.

It was then he realized: *if Erwin can be a pastor, then so can I!*

Ironically, at that very same event I was asking myself if anyone was resonating with what I had to say or if I was just wasting my time. Out of ten thousand people I think there might have been one or two who genuinely connected with how I saw the world and life and faith. Chris Durso was one of them, and sometimes all it takes is one to change the world.

If the only thing that came out of that night was Chris Durso heeding God's call, it was worth my life.

Years later my son, Aaron, was on his own journey of faith and doubt when Chris entered the picture again. Aaron was in New York and running from God. He happened to run into Chris as he was fighting his way back to faith. He immediately loved the Dursos and their gritty and honest approach toward faith.

It was through Aaron that I eventually came to know Chris and his family and became a part of their community.

When we decided to invite our first guest speaker in the twenty-year history of Mosaic here in Los Angeles, it was an easy decision. We called Chris Durso.

The Hollywood scene is a tough one, and our audience is full of skeptics and seekers as well as passionate followers of Christ. Very few people can speak into this space and thrive. There is a demand here for raw honesty and a meaningful message.

Chris has both . . . So does *The Heist.*

The Heist will give you fresh and street-smart language for grace. It will help you understand the work of Jesus in a way that you will know that God is for you! Read on and you will find a book that gives you edgy, accurate, and applicable language for what Jesus has done for us on the cross. It truly is the heist that changes EVERYTHING.

For more than twenty-five years, I have given myself to a beautiful community here in Los Angeles known as Mosaic.

For more than twenty-five years, we have fought the battle of making the church the most relevant and beautiful expression of being human the world has ever known.

For more than twenty-five years, we have believed that one

day a tribe would emerge across the world that would lead the church to become humanity's most creative force.

For more than twenty-five years, we have believed that God will raise up leaders who engage the Scriptures and the culture with fresh perspectives, with passionate hearts, and with a fearless love for humanity.

Chris Durso is part of this new tribe.

He is proof that a new future is emerging and that it's going to be powerful. *The Heist* is his manifesto.

When Jesus walked the road to Emmaus, though His companions could not recognize Him, He told the story of His death and resurrection in such a way that His words burned in their hearts.

My prayer is that everyone who reads these words written to us by Chris Durso would have a similar experience. May his words burn in our hearts as he shares with us the story of Jesus in a way we haven't heard before.

If you're not careful, this book will cause you to fall so deeply in love with Jesus that He will steal your heart away.

What a promise: that grace would rob us of our shame.

Steal away Lord Jesus . . .

Steal away.

Erwin Raphael McManus

Mosaic, Los Angeles

Author, *The Artisan Soul*

INTRODUCTION

I n 2010, God challenged me to preach every message through and in grace. Until that point it was a topic I would cover only from time to time. I wrestled with God because I was concerned that offering grace would give the reckless a free pass to tamper with any of the seven deadly sins and ultimately dishonor God. During this struggle to understand what God was asking me to do, I realized that a true understanding and revelation of grace causes us to live godly lives, turning down temptation and sin of all sorts. A true revelation of grace not only forgives our sin but also makes us want to turn from sin.

Teaching law provides people with boundaries, boundaries they will likely cross, but grace is where we should live. Grace can be found in every book, every story of the Bible, but we are so focused on law that we miss the freedom and restoration only grace provides. How could I not write a book that would bring the kind of freedom that causes you not to want to cross any boundaries? And when you do, grace tells you that you can always turn back. This message hasn't been delivered well, and the truth of the gospel is being warped as Christians berate one another when laws are violated.

The church's reputation as exclusive, bigoted, insensitive, and hypocritical has kept the message of God's love and grace from being properly understood. Self-righteousness, convoluted ideas, and a disconnected understanding of God's grace don't come from people outside of the church; they have to be experienced (given and received) in the church. Christians have long been suffering under doctrines or ideas of judgment. So much so that many refuse or are unable to see grace as the amazing gift it is. Instead of finding refuge and restoration within the walls of the church, the injured are walking away from church communities and, worse, walking away from their relationship with God.

It is time to tune out our misguided views of God and what He thinks about us so we can dial into grace's frequency. It's time to make an adjustment, an adjustment that will put our lives back on course and lead us into our God-given purpose and destiny.

I've called this book *The Heist* because I believe the way God saved us from Satan's grip and frees us from ourselves, from our sin and shame, is nothing short of an incredible heist. By removing shame and blotting out our sin, He gives us the freedom we need to gain a new perspective on our lives, to see the value we have in God's eyes and His plans for us. This was no easy task, and it wasn't a fair one. There is a very scandalous side to how Jesus accomplished our freedom on and through the Cross.

I almost titled this book *The One Crime Jesus Did Commit,* but the powers that be thought it best not to go that route. They felt this title would be offensive, which I liked. The gospel *is* offensive! The Passion story isn't some nice story. It's a brutally violent love story about a shame-filled humanity and the God who loves humanity beyond limit.

When we spend time focusing on the wrong things, we end up saying no to the plans God has for us. But a minor adjustment can turn our failures into our successes. We have to stop focusing on our inadequacies. We have to stop hiding from our purpose because of our fears and insecurities. We have to stop flogging ourselves for making mistakes. We have to learn how to start living in grace.

As you read, you are going to learn to live in the grace God has scandalously made available to you by adjusting how you think about yourself and how you think about God. The fact that God would rob us of our shame just so we can have with Him the type of relationship He wants us to have is pretty sobering. It changes how we think that He thinks about us, and in turn it will change how we think about Him. We will do this by looking at the parable of the prodigal son, which can be found in Luke 15.

I'm unpacking this parable, touching on two points. First, and most obvious, this story is a message for those who have abandoned the faith. I believe they will see that even when they fail, the Father waits. Grace waits for you to be ready; then grace reconciles you back to the Father. Second, this story is a message for believers, the ones who should be shining examples of mercy but are often judgmental instead. Grace isn't merely available to the believer; it is necessary for the believer. This is where it gets a little messy. Grace can seem unfair; we don't deserve it and we can't earn it. We can't do anything but receive it. God gave us His best when we were at our worst, and we'll see that gift as we unpack this parable.

In the story as the prodigal son is returning home, before he gets cleaned up, before he can apologize, before he is back on his father's property, his father sees him and runs to greet him. Is that shocking? It shouldn't be. This *is* the gospel. This is a picture of the love described in John 3:16. God does the work, and all we have to do is receive it.

God has great plans for you, more than you can imagine. But in order for you to move from nothing to abundance, you have to adjust your thinking. It's time to recalibrate how you receive His Word, understand who He is, and believe what grace means to you.

Chapter 1

THE PLAYERS

Who's Who

The greatest trick the devil
ever pulled was convincing the
world he didn't exist.

—Verbal Kint (Kevin Spacey),
The Usual Suspects

Protected by round-the-clock private security and ten layers of security including motion, heat, and light sensors, buried two floors beneath ground level, and placed inside 160 uniquely locked combination lockboxes made of solid steel were incredible quantities of diamonds, gold, and jewelry—an estimated $200 million worth. As impressive as the security systems were, they were no match for Leonardo Notarbartolo, the mastermind behind the diamond heist in Antwerp, Belgium. Notarbartolo and his crew were able to proceed completely undetected as they broke into 123 of those lockboxes over Valentine's Day weekend in 2003. This was no small feat. It required inside information, careful planning, and precision timing.

It is believed that Notarbartolo lived near the diamond center for three years before that weekend in February, building trusted relationships with the people who would eventually be his victims. This trusted member of the community would soon prove that everything is not what it seems. His stakeout gave him a front-row seat to the comings and goings of the security team and the merchants who stored their treasures at the diamond center that boasted about its top-of-the-line security. Planting himself among those he would be robbing was nearly genius. He not only learned all he needed to know about the area and the security system, but it earned him credibility within the community while he studied and plotted against them. This heist was so brilliantly planned and executed it has been dubbed "the heist of the century."

I admit I am fascinated by the skill and gall one would need to successfully plan and execute a heist, especially one of this magnitude. It also makes me wonder, *What would be so valuable that a person would put his life and freedom on the line? A need? Greed? Ego? Thrills?*

THE PLAYERS

I was preparing a message a few years back when I realized the gospel has all the elements of a great heist. There were some parallels to be noted. I began to see Jesus as a mastermind and His three years of ministry as His stakeout. He had been watching, waiting, and planning. Eventually the cross became one of the most powerful tools ever used by a burglar. Like Notarbartolo, Jesus was clear about His purpose, and He remained focused even as Satan himself attempted to derail Him. Fortunately for us, Satan could not stop what Jesus had planned. Nothing would stop Him from pulling off this heist.

Without our permission and against death's will, Jesus plotted His own heist, and no one ever saw it coming. This grand heist wasn't pulled off for Jesus's financial gain. He wasn't looking to get rich quick. He wasn't looking for the thrill of the chase. He was planning on robbing us *for* God.

You are more valuable than you know, and God longs for your affection. He is a jealous God. He wants your heart, your affections, and your worship. God has had His eye on you since the beginning of time, and there is great competition for you. Let's take a step back to catch a glimpse of the players vying for your attention and your worship.

GOD. The Creator. He creates a wondrous place with everything that all living creatures would need to survive and thrive. He gives us life, and in no time at all, we ruin His original plan. We deceive ourselves and try to come up with a better plan, one that doesn't include Him. But God doesn't abandon us or His plan for us. Instead, He comes up with a plan to redeem us and win back our hearts.

He sends His Son (Jesus) to walk this earth and ultimately take back what was stolen from Him: MAN'S WORSHIP and PRAISE. God's mission and Jesus's purpose are that simple: to take back what is rightfully God's. God desires His glory and receives it through the praise, worship, and obedience of mankind, both male and female, young and old.

He knew we could never give Him our praise on our own; we would need His help. He planned to take away sin, shame, and guilt, but He wouldn't go a step beyond that. In other words, He sets us up to find our way to Him, but He does not force us to come to Him. Why? There would be no satisfaction in forcing humanity to turn to Him, so He doesn't make us do anything or give Him anything. He gives us free will to realize our need for Him on our own, and with that understanding comes a desire to freely worship Him.

Can you see why there would be fierce competition for our affections? If the ultimate satisfaction for God comes from our praise, if it's the one thing He wants most from us, then we should not be surprised to hear there is another thief on the prowl looking for the opportunity to steal our praise from us *and* Him.

SATAN. He plots against us. He comes to steal and destroy. He works to sever us from our Creator and plots to make us believe we have no reason to praise, leaving us feeling hopeless and too frustrated or weighed down to pursue our purpose. The worst thing for him is for you and me to be in communion with God, and he knows it. He wants to take what is rightfully ours, what is rightfully God's. He is aware that he cannot get our praise, so he settles for stealing God's praise from us. The master of destruction does this by luring us into sin, then using guilt and shame against us, because guilt and shame will always keep us from praising God. He lures us into sin, then uses deception to convince us we are unworthy of God's purpose, peace, and forgiveness (all of which bring God joy).

Driven by their individual motives, God and Satan have something in common. They are both relentlessly pursuing you, and they will not stop until God returns and Satan is ultimately and permanently condemned to hell.

Please understand that your soul isn't being fought over by two kingdoms. Heaven and hell are not battling it out for you. God and Satan are. Satan does not have a kingdom. He is not coming back for you. He is the prince of this world, and he is using his influence and ancient strategies to keep you from what is rightfully yours, but he cannot stop the kingdom of heaven from coming for you. Can we just get this out of the way right here, at the very beginning? When the kingdom of heaven appears, Satan *will not* rule over hell; he will be a prisoner himself. He will, once and for all, receive his eternal punishment. He is hoping he can get you and me to join him; maybe misery actually does love company.

CAN YOU STEAL WHAT IS ALREADY YOURS?

Is it considered stealing if you are only taking back what is already yours? Yes, it is. The act of stealing is taking something from somebody against his or her will or without his or her knowledge, even if what you steal rightfully belongs to you. When Christ robbed us of our shame, rescuing us from Satan's grasp, He pulled off what really ought to be called "the heist of the centuries." Jesus stole Satan's power without his approval, keys included! (See Revelation 1:18.)

Because Satan is motivated by pride and jealousy, his plan is to ultimately rob God of the praise that is due Him. We give God praise through our verbal praise and worship. We give God praise when our hearts are leaning in, in awe of the One who created us, listening for Him, speaking to Him, when our hearts are acutely aware of their Creator. More important, we also give God praise by fulfilling His predestined purpose for us; His designed purpose for each one of us is to praise Him. Our very lives are praise in motion.

> We look at this Son and see the God who cannot be seen.
> We look at this Son and see God's original purpose in
> everything created. For everything, absolutely everything,
> above and below, visible and invisible, rank after rank
> after rank of angels—*everything* got started in him and
> finds its purpose in him. (Colossians 1:15–17, MSG)

Satan directly attacks God's desire for our lives by convincing us that we are not worthy of our purpose. Let's take a moment here to understand his tactics. Satan uses our mistakes, our sins, and our shortcomings against us. He convinces us that we are not good enough or that we have gone too far from God to do the things God is calling us to do. Added to this internal struggle is Satan's ability to use us against one another. He recruits other Christians, sometimes those closest to us, to point their accusing fingers at us to remind us of how unqualified and unworthy we are of fulfilling our purpose.

The accuser himself gets us to accuse one another within the four walls of the church. He is not powerful enough to make us do anything, but he certainly persuades us to fix our eyes on ourselves or on what the people around us are doing. These distractions or, more clearly stated, this tactic of comparison keeps us from pursuing our purpose. His tactics are timeless, but in this case the saying is true: there is nothing new under the sun. Satan is not a creator; he cannot create, so he cannot devise new tactics against us. His tactics are nothing more than recycled garbage. They may be packaged differently, but at the core they're always the same. His plots are direct and precise, and he uses an arsenal of old tools to separate us from what is rightfully ours. These tricks explain why we can easily relate to some of the biblical heroes of our faith when we read about the mistakes they made and the traps they fell into thousands of years ago.

Knowing full well the tactics Satan would employ against

us, knowing he would come after us with shame, Jesus comes down, becomes sin, and steals the consequences of our shame right out from under us without our permission or knowledge; the violent take it by force.

Until Jesus "was about thirty years old" (Luke 3:23), He walked the earth, fulfilling prophecy. For the next and last three years of His life, He lived among us; Jesus had a front-row seat, a close-up view of the darkness of humanity. He saw sin in action and knew that teenagers needed help; He knew single mothers needed help; He knew married men needed help. He understood all our struggles well. Jesus knew we were in desperate need of His help to overcome every strategic attack from Satan. Just as Leonardo Notarbartolo watched and learned, waiting for the right time to pull off one of the greatest diamond heists of all time, Jesus watched and learned during His time on earth. Jesus was able to pull off "the heist of the centuries" because He took the time to be a part of the world. HE KNEW SIN. HE SAW SIN. HE BECAME SIN.

Jesus went to such extreme measures because He knew there was no way we could have done this for ourselves. In the parable of the prodigal son, we see proof of this. The younger son, the prodigal, could not redeem himself, and we cannot do it for one another either. In the end the father of the prodigal son had to do what his children could not do on their own.

THE PARABLE OF THE PRODIGAL SON

The story of the prodigal son is one you may have heard and read countless times. If you haven't read it, don't worry. Allow me to share some of the highlights with you from Luke 15. The story of the prodigal son is about a father and his two sons. The father is wealthy, and both his sons live with him, enjoying the benefits of their father's wealth. The father has staff to take care of the animals, the property, and all the needs of the house. The younger of the two boys one day asks his father for his inheritance. His father obliges his request, and the son takes his inheritance, leaves the benefits of his home, and over time squanders all his money and has to go back home. Before he makes it to the front door, the father sees him and runs toward him to welcome him back. The father throws a big party to celebrate. While the father and younger son are celebrating, the older son refuses to join the party because he is bitter. He thinks it is unfair for his brother to get this homecoming celebration when he had been so reckless. He compares his own faithfulness to his brother's recklessness and questions his father: Why should his brother get the best celebration when he himself didn't even get a "well done" party? The story ends with the father explaining and justifying his decision to celebrate his sinful son, saying, "Son, you don't understand. You're with me all the time, and everything that is mine is yours—but this is a wonderful time, and we had to celebrate. This brother of yours was dead, and he's alive! He was lost, and he's found!" (Luke 15:31–32, MSG).

The story of the prodigal son is a cautionary tale for Christians. It shows us what a father's love should look like, and it reminds us to be careful about the ideas we entertain and what we are looking at. Otherwise, like the prodigal son, we may forget the benefits of being in our Father's house and end up wandering off, only to find ourselves stripped of anything of value and left all alone.

Could there be more to this story? Are there any players we might have overlooked? If we read too quickly, we will likely miss it. Let's start at the top, in that very first verse of Luke 15, where the scene is set for us. Jesus was not off to the side in a private place and out of sight telling this story to people we would easily consider sinners like the prodigal son. Jesus was out in the open. The Pharisees and the scribes (the religious leaders) were there. The tax collectors were there. They all wanted to hear Jesus tell His stories, but the religious leaders seemed to be increasingly distracted by that day's crowd. They couldn't understand why Jesus, a religious man, would allow tax collectors to sit with Him. How could He be so welcoming to the wicked and out in the open, no less? This was no accident, nor was it a surprise. Jesus had some tactical moves too.

The Pharisees often listened to Jesus's teachings. Sitting with the notorious was nothing new to Jesus; He seemed to attract all kinds of people. He never seemed to shy away from anyone—not the good, the bad, or the ugly—and this day was no different. I am pretty confident Jesus intended for both groups of people to hear this story.

As we read the story, it is clear this parable is about a son who went searching for more than what he could find at home. He was looking around, wondering what he could be missing. I think it is safe to say he spent too much time entertaining those thoughts. He let his imagination run wild, and his daydreams made him forget the benefits of the house he was in: his father's protection, the meals that were available to him, and the support he received. Eventually he left his father's house, and when he returned, he was empty handed and covered in sin.

When we read about his return, our minds' eyes are on him, the sinful son, and rightfully so. But what about Jesus's audience? What did they have to do with this story? There is a clear correlation between the younger brother and the sinners sitting around the table with Jesus, but what about the Pharisees? Is there a correlation between the older brother and the Pharisees? Is it possible that this story isn't just about the young son, the "sinner" who left home?

A FATHER'S LOVE

I have the privilege of being a father. I have two beautiful children. I have a nine-year-old son named Dylan. Dylan wants to travel the world and preach the gospel. I also have a six-year-old daughter named Chloe. Chloe is a character with a smile that will charm the last quarter right out of your pocket. She wants to preach to the nations.

They are very young, and while I have had them in my life for only a few years, I am pretty sure there is nothing they can do that will ever cause me to stop loving them. I want the very best of everything for them. That's just the way it is for most fathers. God is no exception.

God is ultimately motivated by His ferocious love for humanity and His desire for our individual and collective worship, because all glory and honor belong to Him alone. His original plan was for man to live unashamedly so that we would worship and praise Him freely, but the Fall of man changed that. The Fall of man robbed God of what was and is rightfully His. Jesus's sacrifice by way of the cross became the antidote and plan to get all that back. He was only stealing (or taking back) what originally belonged to Him.

You cannot do anything to earn His love, nor can you do anything to lose His love. He was so determined to get you back that He came up with a whole plan that would cost Him His Son.

THE BATTLE IS ON

When we read the story of the prodigal son, we need to under-stand there is a battle between the prodigal son's purpose and the allure of the forbidden. We know his father has provided every-thing a son would need to thrive and live a good life. It is safe to assume the father wants the best for his son, but his heart must also be aching over his son's request for his inheritance.

In the distance I can easily imagine Satan wringing his hands, plotting, scheming, taunting the prodigal son's imagina-tion, working to lure him out of his house and away from the future his father has imagined.

The battleground is not in the house or in a distant land. This battle is taking place in the prodigal son's heart and mind. He knows what is expected, what is required, and what is right, yet he can't help but feel the allure; he's drawn toward the unknown.

This has always been the inner struggle of man. The Bible is full of verses that warn us to guard our hearts and that tell us our hearts are deceitful. If we are going to guard our hearts, we also have to guard our thoughts and our eyes. Otherwise, we run the risk of fixing them on the wrong things, and before we know it, our hearts and souls are dark because we have allowed the wrong things in. Then, like the younger son, we're off wandering, look-ing for something more appealing than what we have at home.

How could someone who knows so much Scripture miss this? We know Satan knows the Bible back and forth. He knows the truth about his opponent: God is omnipotent (all-powerful), omniscient (all-knowing), and omnipresent (everywhere at all times and seeing it all). God doesn't have to ask Satan's permission to go anywhere or do anything. The same is not true for Satan.

Satan has some good tricks up his sleeve, but they are old tricks. He cannot create, so there is nothing new coming from his corner. He also lacks the power of the Holy Spirit. This is key. While Satan can read the text, he cannot decipher the text as we can. He cannot gain revelation from the Holy Spirit as we can, so he cannot truly understand the context the way we can, which renders him less powerful than he would like us to think.

This is why it is so important for us to know the Word of God. Satan doesn't really know or understand it, yet he tries to use it against us. So why then do we, who have the power of the Holy Spirit at work in us, look at Satan as if he were, in any way, shape, or form, God's competition? How do we get stuck when we know Satan is only a master of deception? He is so good he could be deceiving himself.

This tells us more about heaven than we've likely ever considered. Satan's tactics never change. They're always the same. He sits in his corner looking for ways to divide and separate us from God. He lures us into sin by getting us to focus on the big payout, that thing we have to have: the money, the relationship, the good time. Then, like a person abusing an animal, he grabs us by our necks and sticks our noses in the mess we've made. He keeps us looking at our mistakes so we are so busy looking down that we miss the opportunity to see the face of grace looking right at us, waiting for us to realize that grace and freedom from the weight of our guilt and shame are available to us.

It might be important for us to take a few moments to search our hearts and figure out what that deception looks like for us. Satan uses the same strategies against all of us; he only changes his tactics. He will keep the sinner looking at his mistakes (the addiction, the hurt he has caused, the shame she has carried, and so on) because as long as we are looking at our mistakes, we will find it difficult to believe we are worthy of the grace, forgiveness, and the fresh start that await us. Fortunately, it isn't up to us, and there is a master plan in the works to save us from death, shame, and ourselves.

Chapter 2

THE MASTER PLAN

Motive Is Everything

No, God has not rejected and disowned His people [whose destiny] He had marked out and appointed and foreknown from the beginning.

—Romans 11:2, AMPC

Like the prodigal son, Adam and Eve, when they were in the garden, were set up with everything they would ever need. There was food and water; they would have complete dominion, ruling over animals and the land. There was just one rule in the garden: stay away from *that* tree. Adam and Eve failed, and everything from that moment on changed. Adam and Eve, who once walked freely, who once had no care in the world, were now hiding. They felt shame. They were suddenly aware of their nakedness. They felt guilty. They had messed up; they knew it and they could not hide it. God wasn't surprised by their disobedience; He wasn't taken off guard by what they had done. He didn't stand in the garden and wonder what He would do next. He knew exactly what He was going to do. He sought them out; He called them out. But instead of striking them dead, He did something that was the complete opposite. Like the father in the story of the prodigal son, He provided their covering. He took the sting of their nakedness away.

God's original plan for humanity included our covering. He

knew we would need it. Our covering would come with Jesus's death on the cross. His love for His workmanship was so fierce that He not only set us up with what we would need from the beginning, but He also had a plan ready so we could enjoy life abundantly despite our failures and disobedience.

Since God knew we would fail, why didn't He just make us perfect? I would offer three possible reasons why God did not make us perfect:

1. Even if we were perfect, I am pretty sure we would still find a way to mess up.

2. If He had left us without any options, He would essentially have taken away our free will. Ultimately, that would make God a dictator and not the loving Father we know. So instead of giving us perfection, He came up with a plan to take away our shame— shame caused by man, not by God.

3. He wants our worship and praise, but He doesn't want forced praise, because forced praise produces no glory. God wants our genuine praise, because genuine praise brings God genuine glory.

If the moment Christ robbed us of our shame and saved us from sin and death is truly the greatest heist of all time, then He had to have planned ahead. A truly masterful plan is one that anticipates problems and can't be thrown off when things go awry. There's always a backup or contingency plan. This is absolutely true of our salvation. If God's motive is to cover us and offer us grace, He would make sure we are able to receive that—no matter what. God knew we would mess up, but He still wants us to step into paradise with Him, so He does what any good father would do: He allows us to see how we would mess up on our own. This way, when we ask the million-dollar question, "Why didn't God just make us perfect?" we would know why.

FREE WILL MAKES OUR WORSHIP SWEETER

In order for us to give God the sweet worship He longs for and deserves, we need the same kind of covering Adam and Eve received. Grace is that covering. Grace gives you and me immediate access to a holy God in our current state, but grace does not first appear on the scene in Bethlehem or at Calvary. Far too many Christians believe that grace is a New Testament concept. The truth is, grace makes an appearance in the very first book of the Bible. In Genesis, grace covers Adam and Eve in their naked state, and again when the rest of humanity grieved God's heart, Noah finds grace in the eyes of the Lord.

The first mention of the word *grace* in the Bible shows us that where there is anger and remorse, we find grace. And God's motive is not covert. He has a plan to rescue and save all of us. No exceptions.

> And GOD saw that the wickedness of man was great in
> the earth, and that every imagination of the thoughts of
> his heart was only evil continually. And it repented the
> LORD that he had made man on the earth, and it grieved
> him at his heart. And the LORD said, I will destroy man
> whom I have created from the face of the earth; both
> man, and beast, and the creeping thing, and the fowls of
> the air; for it repenteth me that I have made them. But
> Noah found grace in the eyes of the LORD. (Genesis
> 6:5–8, KJV)

This is, in fact, the first time we read the word *grace* in the Bible, but it is not the first time we experience grace in the Bible. It is the first time *grace* appears in the text, but it is not the first time grace shows up in the text. As I mentioned in chapter 1, grace continually appears throughout the Bible, from the Old Testament to the New.

Fully understanding how man fell is to really accept God's stance. When we have a revelation of grace, we understand two very important truths: we do not deserve to be here, but because of grace we can be here. While I am here, I am going to make it my business to obey God. I am never going to offer anyone the opportunity to intentionally sin. I will not throw stones at my brother or sister, because I know I don't want anyone throwing them at me. This can only happen when we have a revelation of grace.

Did you catch the tension between verses 5 and 8? Are you blown away by the fact that God's sorrowful eye sat in the very same place where Noah found grace? This fact *isn't* because this was the inception of grace but because Noah found himself staring into the eternal source of grace! God's hope from the very beginning was to share the plan.

———

Smart criminals protect themselves by keeping their ideas to themselves. They have their heists all mapped out, but they do not share their notes or the details of their plans with anyone. Leonardo Notarbartolo did not share his plans with anyone; he kept his recon missions and all the details to himself until the time was right. God didn't follow that approach with His master plan. This is what makes God so big. His ability and desire to extend grace to every single one of us is what makes Him the ultimate Mastermind. This may be too big for us to understand, but we don't have to understand it; we just need to accept it as true. He doesn't keep *His* plan a secret. He doesn't hide all His ideas until the last possible minute. He shows us the plan from the very beginning, and He maps it out for us because He wants us to understand His plan well.

Grace is at the center of God's plan for us. When Adam and Eve disobeyed God, grace was present. In the moments that followed, as they realized they were naked, we see the perfect word picture of Romans 5:20.

> God's law was given so that all people could see how
> sinful they were. But as people sinned more and more,
> God's wonderful grace became more abundant. (NLT)

God didn't leave Adam and Eve in the garden alone, ignore them altogether, or wipe them off the face of the earth right then and there, because where sin abounds, grace abounds all the more, and it keeps giving. This is no different than what most parents do. When children mess up, when they leave the safety of the parameters that were set, parents will oftentimes impose additional rules to keep their children safe. The rule set in the garden, the laws Moses later received, and the guidelines we find throughout the Bible do not negate or replace grace; they're not the backup plan for the backup plan. God's plan was to meet our shortcomings with grace, and the temporary laws on earth magnify our need for a lifetime of grace.

It didn't take very long for us to fall short. It happened in the first family, and we also continually fall short. It raises the question: If God knew Adam and Eve would choose the wrong thing, why then would He allow them in the garden in the first place? If He knew you and I would make as many bad choices as we have, why would He give us life? Why would He call us?

Why would He give us purpose, knowing full well that at some point we would all trip and fail? The answer is as simple and as complicated as the question. God allowed them in the garden because we needed free will, and when Adam and Eve eventually failed, God wasn't surprised. He was prepared and responded by confronting them with grace as He covered both Adam and Eve (see Genesis 3:21).

Scripture shows us that we are all bound to sin. In our humanity it is not possible to be perfect. God's law was given to us so that all people could see how sinful we are. "But as people sinned more and more, God's wonderful grace became more abundant." Grace flows from a well that cannot run dry. It hasn't expired. Grace was not limited to Old Testament stories or New Testament parables. God's grace is a present-day gift available to all of us: the sinner and the saint, the child who leaves and the child who stays, the one who runs to sin and the one who makes every effort to do the right thing.

The funny thing about me is that while I believe with all my heart that grace is freely given and readily available, this wasn't always the case. I grew up believing the opposite to be true, that I had to work for forgiveness. I'm not sure why. I never read it in a book, my pastors (who are also my parents) never said anything like this, and yet this is what I believed. I'm a PK (pastor's kid), but that didn't give me a free pass from guilt, so I tried my best never to put myself in a compromising position.

Some of you can identify with me. We are acutely aware of our surroundings at all times. We go to church on Sunday, look around, and feel comfortable. We can enjoy the music when the band is on point. We notice the speaker is eloquent. We know this is the right place for us, but we also think we ought not be here. The shameful details are still too fresh. It's Sunday morning, and we know exactly where we were on Friday night. We know what we were doing yesterday and the person we were doing it with. There's no escaping our truth. The people sitting around us may not know it, but we know the details all too well, and guilt is sitting right there with us, keeping us from giving God any kind of worship.

I remember being in church on one particular Sunday, standing next to my mom and feeling overwhelmed with guilt and fear. The day before I had hung out with some friends at a park, and I smoked a cigarette with them. From the moment I left that park, I was not only completely guilt-ridden, but I was also paranoid. I spent the next fourteen hours or so thinking about what I had done and questioning whether or not God was now done with me. I thought this "sin" was so great that God would not, and could not, forgive me.

As I stood there next to my mom, while the rest of the people were singing and lifting their hands, I was a complete mess. I was overwhelmed by guilt and fear. This was the wrong time to be in church because it was too close to the last time I messed up. It was the wrong time because I imagined God was looking down at me from heaven saying, *Who does he think he is? He can't come to My house after doing what he just did.* I was convinced God was sitting on His throne, shaking His head, and saying, *How could you?* I was sure of one thing: God had to be upset with me.

In our humanity this line of thinking makes perfect sense. It is logical. If someone we are in a relationship with continually disappoints us, then we might decide to cut that person off. We would be right, or justified, in being angry and hurt, but we have to be careful about applying this human logic to a supernatural God. If we view God this way, then we have a faulty perception of God. He is not sitting up in heaven wagging His finger at us. We do not annoy God, nor is He embarrassed by us. He is not angry at you, not even just a little bit. He is mad *about* you. He is looking at you and me with eyes of love.

I didn't have a clear understanding of grace and couldn't handle what I was feeling, so I grabbed my mom by the arm and led her out of the building. It was confession time. Even then, my confession was less about *becoming* right and more about *doing* what was right. I thought there were certain steps I had to take to receive forgiveness; I thought there was something I had to do in order to be forgiven. I didn't want to tell my mom, but I did so because I needed to be sure that I was forgiven and that God and I were still on good terms. Being on good terms with

God didn't just mean I could feel better at that moment; being on good terms with God was also my way of working on my future. Getting right with God meant I was securing a happy life, preserving my calling, and making sure He was saving a beautiful wife for me. I needed to guarantee my entrance into heaven. In my mind it made perfect sense to confess because I had too much at stake.

Some of you understand my logic. You think that you can no longer do the things you were going to do or that you were supposed to do for God. You have given up and packed up your dream as if God weren't already aware of all the ways you would fall short. In Romans we read that God *foreknew* every mistake you would make, and yet He still called you. You were designated as a key part of God's master plan long before you were born. You cannot be dismissed because you have made some bad decisions. We are an integral part of building God's kingdom on earth, and God made space for us in His plans with the full knowledge that you and I would mess up. We still have purpose, despite our failures and slipups. When we make a mistake, God does not turn to the angels in heaven and say, "Did you see that? Why didn't I see that coming? Oh, he definitely can't be a pastor now!" It sounds ridiculous when we say that out loud, but when we disqualify ourselves, that is in essence what we are saying. This is why we have to hide His words and promises in our hearts. When Satan comes at you (because you know he will), you can stand up in the same way Jesus did as Satan attempted to derail His purpose. You can remind Satan exactly what God says about you and what God says about Himself. You are a part of a larger story, and regardless of how you fall, you *still* have your purpose.

A truly masterful plan uses the right people. It's all about whom you know and using the right people to get the job done. When God set out to rob us of our shame and set us free, it was no small undertaking, and the fact is that the human race didn't always listen to or trust God's voice in the matter. The downside of free will is that sometimes we choose wrong. It has happened throughout history, and there are countless examples of it in the Bible. One of the most famous has to do with a man named Noah.

But of that day and hour no one knows, not even the angels of heaven, but My Father only. But as the days of Noah were, so also will the coming of the Son of Man be. For as in the days before the flood, they were eating and drinking, marrying and giving in marriage, until the day that Noah entered the ark, and did not know until the flood came and took them all away, so also will the coming of the Son of Man be. Then two men will be in the field: one will be taken and the other left. Two women will be grinding at the mill: one will be taken and the other left. Watch therefore, for you do not know what hour your Lord is coming. (Matthew 24:36–42, NKJV)

During those early years in that corner of the world, Noah was the guy to know. He was the guy you wanted to know if you wanted to be saved from the flood that was going to wipe away all mankind. The only problem was that people were so caught up in their sinful lifestyles that they weren't even aware trouble was coming their way. God was sending a massive flood to cover the earth, and He had called Noah to build a boat large enough to carry His children safely.

Noah was the man with the plan and the information, but the people in Noah's community completely ignored the warnings that came from watching Noah spend nearly 120 years building a giant boat based on the faith that came from Noah hearing a word from God. Can you imagine how differently things might have turned out had those people simply repented and followed after God?

This gives us a glimpse into the mind of the Master. His goal was to get His plan for us from His mind to ours, and while this may be difficult to understand, He created us in such a way that we would actually understand it enough to act.

Why do we read the story of Noah and feel great sadness for the people who weren't in the boat, but then when we look at our own lives, we are doing almost the same thing? We hear what

God tells us, we see His plan for us and for humankind as a whole, but we delay in making the necessary corrections to our behavior. Why is it that we wish the people around Noah would have followed God when we don't ourselves? Taking God's kindness and grace for granted was a form of evil then, and it is a form of evil today.

How many of us show up at church on Sunday or are serving in a ministry while we are still holding on to sin? How often do we make excuses to do anything but what God has called us to do?

"Nah, but, Pastor, I need to do my thang!"

"I'm too young."

"I'm old enough to know what I can and cannot handle."

"The Bible has too many restrictions. No person can follow all those rules!"

"No way does that still apply today."

"I need my freedom."

Interestingly enough, true freedom is not found in our ability to run wild and do our own "thang." True freedom is only found within the parameters God sets. We seem to think God wants to restrict us and keep us from something, when the truth is that our freedom in Him is not contingent on our physical circumstances. That's another lie Satan would have us believe. He gets us worried about what *we* cannot do, because when we are focused on what we cannot do, we miss out on what only

God can do. This is why you can physically be in a prison and still be free and on fire for Jesus. In the midnight hour, shackled up in their prison chains, Paul and Silas worshiped God (see Acts 16:25).

It is worth highlighting that Paul and Silas did not worship God out of obligation or to gain their freedom. Paul and Silas worshiped God because while their bodies were not free, they were free. When you are facing a tough situation, I would challenge you to follow suit. We cannot allow our circumstances to bind and keep us from the freedom that worship provides. In fact, there is freedom in your worship because "where the Spirit of the Lord is, there is freedom" (2 Corinthians 3:17, ESV).

The truth of the master plan that God has set before us is that while the road can be tough, God has set out something wonderful for us. When we ignore the plan, when we hear God calling us one way and we go the other, we're waving off the one thing that can truly set us free—grace. Friend, I hope this truth sets you free from some stuff today and gives you the freedom to give God what He longs for: your worship. God will always make room for those who make room for Him. He accomplishes in the supernatural what we could never accomplish in the physical.

Let's go back to Noah. The ark he built was massive. It had to carry his family and two of every animal. However, I wonder if there was also room left on that boat for those who would have turned from their evil ways and followed God. Was Noah called to build such a massive boat only to ride in it with his family and the animals God called him to bring, or was God instructing Noah to make a boat that had visible space for any prodigals? After all, God gave Noah the specifics for the space he was building. Noah wasn't an architect nor was he a designer, but the Mastermind gave him a complete plan and told Noah exactly how to execute it.

Since He is concerned about the birds of the air and the fish of the sea, how much more concerned is He about you? The kingdom of God will never reject anyone who approaches it properly. Jesus Christ is inclusive to all and exclusive to none. Why? Because of the promise God made: "*Everyone* who calls on the name of the Lord shall be saved" (Romans 10:13, NRSV).

This story of Noah is one of the greatest depictions of God's love. This is the gospel, and this is why the story ends on a promise.

The promises of God are unbreakable, no matter how many promises you make and break yourself. This is a key point to know, because after the flood is over, God promises never to flood the earth again.

[God said,] "This is my promise to you: *All life* on the earth was destroyed by the flood. But that will never happen again. A flood will never again destroy all life on the earth."

And God said, "I will give you something to prove that I made this promise to you. It will continue forever to show that I have made an agreement with you and every living thing on earth. I am putting a rainbow in the clouds as proof of the agreement between me and the earth. When I bring clouds over the earth, you will see the rainbow in the clouds. (Genesis 9:11–14, ERV)

Unlike you and me, when God makes a promise, you can be sure He is going to keep it! Now I know what you're thinking: *I don't make promises I can't keep!* Or maybe you think you're too smart to fall for the obviously ridiculous promises. Do any of these shady promises sound familiar?

"If you take these diet pills, you will lose twenty pounds in ten days."

"If you wear this cologne, every woman on earth will be immediately drawn to you."

"If you go to sleep right now, I'll give you twenty dollars in the morning."

"I will never lie to you again."

"I am never going to eat like that again."

This isn't how God operates. He never makes empty promises. And not only does God come through on all His promises, but He goes over the top to fulfill His promises!

God doesn't just make a promise; He gives us a rainbow as a symbol and reminder of the promise He has made to us. Yet that doesn't seem to be enough for Him. God knew that even though a rainbow is a good start, He needed to give us an even greater symbol of hope. And while a symbol of hope was good, a figure of hope would be even better. He knew the perfect guy. Through this man, God would make a great promise.

I'm not talking about Noah. Noah is just a foreshadowing of the One I'm referring to. I'm talking about the greater Noah, the soon-and-coming King. Jesus Christ is the man to know!

God planned on Jesus's taking human form for you. This moment in time, this book, it's all FOR YOU, because He knew you couldn't do it without Him. Today you can find this guy because this guy, Jesus, made Himself available to us.

> For all the promises of God find their Yes in him [Jesus].
> That is why it is through him that we utter our Amen to
> God for his glory. (2 Corinthians 1:20, ESV)

All God's promises are fulfilled through Christ. The guy you want to know today is Jesus. Jesus allows us to know that we all can be saved, and because of Him, we have these promises of

God's grace and salvation. The Old Testament promises never to flood the earth again. The New Testament is *proof* that no one ever has to drown again! To say yes to God is to say yes to accepting the plan. That is what a mastermind does; he not only gets you to accept the plan, but he gets you to participate in the plan.

While Notarbartolo's thirty years of experience as a burglar made him a mastermind in his own right, his plan was flawed; his success as a thief was contingent on the rest of his team's performance. They could not afford to make one mistake or the whole thing would come undone. Grace's plan is foolproof, because even though you and I will mess up, we don't have to pay the price for any of it. Grace will cover it all.

Chapter 3

THE VICTIMIZED

"It Makes Sense to Me, So It Must Be Right!"

These voices, these voices,
I hear them
And when they talk,
I follow, I follow.

—Eminem, "Guilty Conscience"

When I read the interviews with Leonardo Notarbartolo, I detected a confident man. He spoke very matter-of-factly about the first time he pulled a heist; he was only six years old. He knew he was good at it, and in his adult years he says he believes he was born to be a thief. With years of experience under his belt, he knew what it would take to pull off a good heist. He knew what would work and what wouldn't. He knew it would require time to plan and time to prepare his crew. He worked with his five-man crew planning, revising, doing mock run-throughs, organizing tools and materials. He was determined to successfully break through the ten layers of security systems. He walked through every possible scenario with his crew. He watched every move the security team made, he noted the times deliveries were made, and he noticed how the merchants and customers moved in and out of the area. For three years he moved among the people. He rented office space in that building; he made an effort to get to know the men on the security team and the other jewelers in the building. He wanted to be a familiar, unsuspected face, and he wasn't sloppy or hurried. His charisma and friendliness were the secrets to his success in his thirty years of criminal activity. While our prisons may be filled with people who hurried through botched robberies, Notarbartolo had his eye on the prize and was meticulous, disciplined, and as careful as he could be because he was determined to break into that vault and steal whatever he could manage to pull out of there.

ENTITLEMENT: DO I HAVE ENOUGH?

The parable of the prodigal son starts with the younger of two sons asking his father for what he thinks he has a right to have, and he wants it right now. The problem isn't wanting what would have eventually been rightfully his. The problem is wanting it before the time is right.

There's a television show I used to watch as a kid about a family with five children. The parents navigate the preteen, teenage, and college years like professional tag-team wrestlers. I remember one episode when one of the daughters wants to hang out with the wrong crowd. It's the wrong crowd because they are all underage, but they figure out a way to get some alcohol, and they drink. She doesn't just drink; she gets drunk. The parents want to teach her a lesson, so they get the youngest sister involved. They pretend to play a drinking game. The older sister watches the younger sister drink what appears to be alcohol (it was tea), and she soon acts like she's drunk. The older sister doesn't think it is cool or funny to watch her little sister drink. In fact, she is really upset about this game. The older sister eventually figures out that they were teaching her a lesson, but as she watched her sister's behavior change, she realized how dangerous it is to get something before you are ready to handle the responsibility that comes with it.

When the prodigal son requested his inheritance, the request wasn't just unnecessary, ridiculous, and outlandish. This request was hurtful and insulting. He was pretty much telling his father, "I can't wait for you to die, so just give me what you've worked hard for, and let me enjoy it now." Not only was he not ready for such a huge responsibility; he was essentially telling his father that he didn't need him anymore and that his own plans were better than anything his dad had for him.

What motivates a child, the baby of the house, to ask his father for something he hasn't himself earned? His only right to it would have been after the father had passed away. I can't imagine what would go through a man's heart and mind as his son made this request. The boy he's nurtured, loved, and provided for all his life now wants what is not yet rightfully his. What would justify asking for his inheritance while his father was still alive?

An inheritance is the money or possessions a person receives *after* the death of another individual, when the individual no longer has any use for it, after open debts are taken care of, funeral arrangements are made and paid for, servants are paid, and the first-born son receives his portion. The younger son is assuming his need for his cut now is more important than all the standard responsibilities and, even worse, anything his father might need between this moment and the actual moment of his death.

Let me be clear here. While asking for an advance on an inheritance is rude in any culture, it was especially insulting in this corner of the world. There were laws about how these things were handled. Jesus's audience knew just how offensive this request was. I can almost hear them gasp two lines into this story.

Jesus went on to say that the son moved quickly, which means the father immediately complied. I wonder what this heartbroken father was really thinking. Was it not worth fighting over, or was this the perfect setup for a teachable moment?

I remember being left alone for the first time as a teenager. My parents had to be at an event for church, and they would be gone until later in the evening. This was the first time I was responsible for dinner. They gave me instructions and options, but instead of making a sandwich, ordering pizza, or warming up leftovers as I was instructed to do, I ate ice cream. It wasn't my original plan, but it seemed like a good idea at the time. Deciding to eat ice cream for dinner wasn't the worst idea in the world. Eating three full portions, which made me incredibly sick, made this the worst option for dinner. When I came up with the idea, it seemed brilliant, but once I executed it, it almost executed me. Did I mention that I am lactose intolerant?

Sin does that too. From a distance just about anything can look appealing. You want that relationship, that position, that house, that job. Whatever it is, that thing is calling you day and night, night and day. You want it so much you almost become consumed by it. You think about it so long that you do whatever it takes to get it, but once you have it, you realize it wasn't so great, and now you have to deal with the consequences: bankruptcy, compromised integrity, a trashed reputation, the guilt, the shame.

Did you eventually find yourself trying to figure out how you got into this mess in the first place? Oh, the irony when the thing we are running to becomes the thing we are eventually running from.

I wonder what the prodigal son thought he was missing out on. We could look at his life and assume he had everything a man could hope for, need, and want. He had money, a nice house with servants, and a father who loved him. What could he have been missing? What could have caught the prodigal son's eye when he finally decided to take his inheritance and leave his father, and how long had he been daydreaming about it? I think we have all done it.

We can see the wandering eye in cartoons also. I'm reminded

of Disney's movie *The Lion King.* Remember the scene where Mufasa and Simba are sitting at the top of the mountain? The father and son are overlooking a serene kingdom, and Mufasa tells Simba that his kingdom is everything the light touches.

Simba's curiosity is piqued. Mufasa is casting a vision for his son and sharing his dream. He wants his son to have full access to the kingdom, but he is also setting up some parameters to keep Simba safe. For Mufasa, the darkness represented evil, but for Simba, the darkness represented the unknown. The darkness wasn't necessarily evil to Simba; it was simply unknown. And the unknown can often seem far more enticing than what we know, regardless of how good we have it.

Simba is no different from most children; we question whether or not our parents really do know best. We would do well to choose to be obedient and live within the confines of the warnings or parameters, but that doesn't always happen.

For Simba, staying confined to the places he could see was too limiting. For the prodigal son, staying confined to a home he knew too well, with the expectation of an inheritance, took away all the mystery and the adventure. He did not want a predictable life. He was young, and he was sure he was missing out on some good times. If you're like me, someone who loves spontaneity, you don't want to live in a box, wondering what else is out there. Life should feel like an adventure.

There are some instances when we know a father knows

best, but sometimes this logic is too simple. This was the problem for the prodigal son. Had he just been greedy, knowing that he shouldn't be asking for his inheritance, he would have tried to steal it and run away in the middle of the night without anyone knowing. But because he was also entitled, he bravely asked for his inheritance and proudly stood around waiting for it.

It seems that Simba experienced what the prodigal son was feeling when he asked for his inheritance. What he had was not enough; he wanted more. Simba didn't want to experience just the land that the light touched; he also wanted to explore the land that the light didn't touch. He wanted to explore the great unknown, the untapped resources that could possibly make him richer. Was the grass greener, taller? How much better was life just past the boundaries set before him? This is one of the greatest lies of the Enemy: he convinces us that what we have isn't enough and that what we don't have is exactly what we need. He tricks us into believing that we are somehow victims and that we can't have it all. We see this from the Fall of man and all throughout the Bible. The truth, however, is there are some things better left in the dark, unseen and untouched.

> Your eyes are windows into your body. If you open your
> eyes wide in wonder and belief, your body fills up with
> light. If you live squinty-eyed in greed and distrust, your
> body is a dank cellar. If you pull the blinds on your

windows, what a dark life you will have! (Matthew
6:22–23, MSG)

What thoughts could the prodigal son have been entertaining? What daydreams were dancing around in his mind? Had he
been sitting in the sun too long, staring into the distance, imagining life just beyond his father's property line? Maybe his friends
were telling him about all the things he was missing out on by
staying home being a good son: the wild parties, the wild ladies,
the nightlife, the adventures.

The fact of the matter is that we don't know exactly what
caused the prodigal son to leave his home; we can only speculate.
Some would suggest he was guilty of greed, but it could have
been any one of the other seven deadly sins that drew him away:
pride, lust, envy, sloth, gluttony, or wrath. This may be a stretch
because the Bible doesn't spell out his motive. What we do know
is that all these sins have driven humanity to do far worse than
run away and squander an inheritance.

None of us is exempt from the lies that Satan uses to lure us
away from the safety or covering God provides. Let's not forget
that while the prodigal's father may have been giving his sons
everything they could have needed or wanted, there was still one
lying in wait, plotting against the son and his father's purpose.
Satan was likely teasing this young man with all the what-ifs you
and I have entertained. Whatever the sin, no matter how big or

how small, this one truth still remains: no sin was powerful enough to disqualify the prodigal from receiving what God wanted for him, and it definitely wasn't powerful enough to keep God from getting His glory.

This is why Jesus is guilty of pulling off this heist, because we fall into the traps Satan sets, and we take on sin that is too heavy for us to carry.

Whatever the allure, it somehow was so appealing that the prodigal son arrived at the conclusion that asking for his inheritance, breaking his father's heart, and giving up what he had at home was the right thing for him to do. Can we really be mad at him, though? We've all been there. We have all been guilty of thinking that what we have isn't enough, and we risk it all to get what we want. You want those shoes so badly you'll pay only half of your utility bills this month so you can buy the shoes while hoping the electric company doesn't shut off your lights. Or you skip taking a very important midterm test because going to *that* concert or *that* basketball game with *that* person is just the opportunity you've been waiting for and dreaming about.

Focusing on a goal is not necessarily a bad thing. We should set our sights on things we need or want and then make decisions that will move us toward that goal or desire. That's why we skip fancy dinner dates so we can save up for dream vacations and why we skip junk food just before beach season is upon us. When our eyes are on a goal, we are somehow able to make sacrifices and adjustments to reach that goal.

We just need to be careful about whom or what we are focusing on and the things (or relationships) we set aside to get them. The worst place to look is away from the Father. This was the prodigal son's issue. This is why he left his house. He thought there was more out there for him than his father had to offer, and he wanted it now. Satan has been baiting humanity with this very issue since the garden, and until we realize it's a trap, we will fall for it. Every. Single. Time. Jesus warns us to keep our eyes wide open. If we're thinking too small and forget about the bigger picture, we can make decisions that will lead us to dark places, where the grass is not greener.

When we spend too much time thinking about the stuff that's just out of our view, the things we don't have, the adventures in the dark areas, or how we compare to others, we can trick ourselves into thinking we have earned or deserved the right to explore these things and that nothing should stand in our way of getting them. That's where the quest for adventure becomes a quest into danger.

AM I ENOUGH?

The prodigal son went looking outside of his home for happiness. He wasn't satisfied being the responsible son. He thought what he saw outside of his own life would benefit him, but in the end it hurt him, and it hurt God. This is an extreme example of what sin does. It makes life outside of God's plan for us look appealing; it makes running away look like a good idea, but we eventually find out it can destroy us.

What about how we see ourselves? How does our perception of ourselves fit into the big picture? Do we see beauty? Do we see pain? Do we see an incomplete picture? We have to be careful about the filters we use when we are looking at ourselves, and at one another for that matter. It can be destructive to spend too much time looking at our mistakes, our sins, our past choices, and our shame. This is another area where Satan gets pretty sneaky. He gets us to fix our eyes all over the place: we look at one another, we look at our past, we look at our beauty, but we don't look at the one thing God has set His eyes on.

> The LORD does not look at the things people look at.
> People look at the outward appearance, but the LORD
> looks at the heart. (1 Samuel 16:7)

The author is clear here. While we look at people's faces, God looks at our hearts. He looks at you with both love and kindness. It doesn't even matter what your face or heart actually looks like. He simply wants your face and heart focused on Him alone, because He knows that looking any other direction will lead you away from Him.

There are many stories in the Bible that show us how destructive it is to individual lives when we believe what others say when they look at us. Take Pharaoh and the Israelites. After Pharaoh finally gives in to Moses's nagging about letting the Israelites go, he realizes he has made a mistake because he will have no one to do his backbreaking work in Egypt. So he rounds up some troops to catch them and bring them back. Pharaoh isn't able to reach them because God closes up the Red Sea behind the Israelites, but what the Israelites believe about themselves goes with them all the way to the Promised Land. Forty years later they get to Canaan, and when they realize there will be challenges ahead, they get angry. I can't imagine what they expected when they finally arrived: a red carpet, the welcome wagon? Whatever it was, when they arrive at the city gate and it looks like it is going to be too hard for them to enter, they are angry. The Bible tells us the entire community was complaining. They wondered, "Why didn't we die in Egypt? . . . Why don't we just head back to Egypt?" (Numbers 14:2–3, MSG). They looked at one another and saw nothing more than a large group of slaves. They believed the lie Pharaoh had sold them all those years before. They were slaves. How often do we believe the lies we are told by people who are looking at our outward appearance?

This isn't an ancient, biblical problem. This is a very real problem today. With people heading to plastic surgeons, dermatologists, and otolaryngologists in huge numbers, we're a generation of people looking to fix and perfect our outward appearance. People are so worried about being judged by their appearance or physical qualities and hating them so much that they are willing to spend money to fix them has led to big business.

You are enough. You just have to believe it and be brave enough to step into it. You have to take the time to refocus your eyes. What is your heart saying? How can you bring your heart and your thoughts into alignment with what God says about you?

DIVISION IN THE HOUSE

I wonder what life was like in the prodigal son's home before he ran away. Were the brothers constantly fighting, as brothers often do? Was the younger brother tired of always playing second fiddle to an older, more responsible brother? Did he grow up hearing, "Why can't you be more like your brother?" Living in the shadow of a smarter, older brother would have been tough. Is that what caused him to want to leave his house so badly? Or did he think he was missing out on something? Was he comparing his life to what the guys down the street were doing? Did he start believing the lies? Perhaps he had been counting the days until he could collect his inheritance and be done with both his father and his brother, and he just got tired of waiting.

> If My people who are called by My name put away their pride and pray, and *look for My face,* and turn from their sinful ways, then I will hear from heaven. I will forgive their sin, and will heal their land. (2 Chronicles 7:14, NLV)

When our souls are longing for more, the last thing we need to do is look around to see what other people have or what they're doing. That's where the prodigal son went wrong. That may be why he left his house. That may be why he abandoned the safety of his father's covering. He foolishly thought there was more for him to experience than what his father could offer; he couldn't resist.

The reality is that this is not an Old Testament or a New Testament problem. This is not a biblical problem. This is the trap that has been set for all humanity over and over again. Satan has been baiting us with this very issue since the first family was planted in the garden. The problem for us is that we all do it. We focus on the wrong thing much of the time.

Too often we wonder what we're missing out on, and our eyes start to wander. We assume there has to be something better *outside of* the house, so we entertain the question, "What am I missing?" We doubt God's sovereignty and the goodness of His plan for us, we doubt the power behind the grace He offers us, and we walk away from what God has for us. No one is exempt from this temptation, not you and definitely not me.

The prodigal son collected his share and took off for a distant country, where he spent all his inheritance. If he had used some of that energy to seek God in the midst of his confusion or frustration, if he had tried to talk to God about the void he was feeling, then he might not have grabbed his money and run off.

Chapter 4

THE RUNAWAY

Anywhere but Here

You don't make up for your sins in church. You do it in the streets. You do it at home.

—Charlie (Harvey Keitel), *Mean Streets*

If there is one thing we can learn from the prodigal son's experience so far, it is how Satan makes us think we are missing out on something. He will feed us lies that cause us to make a detour in search of what we might be missing. I would imagine the prodigal's decision wasn't made overnight. I wonder how long he was wondering about what he was missing out on or how many times he packed a bag to leave, only to unpack again. He must have been sitting with this uneasiness for some time.

Unsatisfied with his life, the son somehow forgot about the benefits of his house, the benefits of living with a father who seemed to provide everything the son needed, the benefits of the warm home, the meals the staff served him. He lost sight of what was real and what was right in front of him. Satan must have painted a picture to suggest anywhere would be better than there. In this case, he got the prodigal son not only to leave the safety of his home and the covering of his father but also to walk away from his purpose.

How often do we do the same thing? We forget about the

benefits of where we are, the benefits of being in the house, and we start romanticizing all the places that have to be better. Somehow, instead of being a place of safety, the house becomes a threat, and that threat was the very thing that drew the son toward the adventures that were out there just waiting for him. He packed his belongings, including his inheritance, and he essentially ran away from home.

Think back to Leonardo Notarbartolo and the careful planning that went into pulling off the most amazing diamond heist in history. The men Notarbartolo worked with had to keep their eyes on the prize and trust that Notarbartolo's plan would ultimately get them something so amazing that it would be worth the waiting and the meticulous work. It's the same with us. Christ's plan for us, His ultimate goal of robbing us of shame and setting us free, is wonderful. However, it takes work and time, and it means we have to spend our days focused on what God has for us even if something outside of God's will might be more satisfying in the moment.

WHAT IS RIGHT
INSTEAD OF THE RIGHT NOW

A house is a refuge and a place of safety. It's an authority and a home base. Of course, sometimes our homes can go from feeling like an anchor that keeps us steady to being a weight pulling us down. For the prodigal son, his home had started to feel like an anchor, and he ran away in search of something great. Of course at other times things and people in our homes really are there to pull us down. That was the case for Joseph.

Joseph worked in the home of a high-ranking Egyptian official named Potiphar. Joseph was placed there, he worked there, and God promoted him in that house. That home was where God intended Joseph to be, and by serving the house faithfully, Joseph was doing as God asked. However, there was someone else in the home who was intent on straying from the path a bit: Potiphar's wife.

Joseph was purpose driven; Potiphar's wife was not. She seemed to have lost sight of her role and her position in the house. She had everything she needed, yet she wanted more: Joseph. I can't judge her for it. After all, it's human nature. We are drawn to the things we're not supposed to touch. It's what Adam and Eve did in the garden. They were told not to eat from the tree, yet Eve was hanging around it and before you knew it, she and Adam had both eaten its fruit. Joseph was wise to turn Mrs. Potiphar down each time she propositioned him, but somehow she wasn't discouraged. She was determined to get what she shouldn't have, all because she wanted it, so she continued to attempt to seduce Joseph in her own house.

Before we judge her, let's understand the source of her rebellion. Her desire to run toward the wrong thing probably came from her own dissatisfaction. Maybe Potiphar stopped paying attention to her. Maybe he was cheating on her, and she knew all about it. Some commentators suggest he was a eunuch; maybe she was unsatisfied in her marriage. I'm sure her life was full of glamour in some areas, probably to make up for the areas that were not so glamorous. Maybe she was simply attracted to who Joseph was. The Bible actually notes that Joseph was "well-built and handsome" (Genesis 39:6), so it is quite possible she saw in him what she hadn't found in her husband. While I think it is important to understand how she was feeling, I want to be careful not to suggest her behavior was justifiable. Noticing Joseph was attractive wasn't necessarily wrong. Spending too much time looking at him, daydreaming, and ultimately pursuing him is where she got herself into trouble. Like the prodigal son, she imagined something outside of her marriage was more appealing than what she actually had in her marriage and in her house.

But I'm not making her out to be a monster. She probably spent plenty of time justifying her desires. As she spent time thinking about what she felt she was lacking, it probably made perfect sense to her to find someone else to fulfill the needs she had—her need to be wanted, loved, appreciated, validated. Who's to say that Joseph didn't feel anything toward her and that he didn't want to sleep with her too? If we remember they were human, like you and me, then we know her motivations were not very different than ours, and it is possible for Joseph to have been attracted to her also. As the wife of the chief of security, she likely had access to exotic floral baths, aromatic perfumes, and skin-softening oils. She probably spent some time every day making sure she looked good. The difference, however, between Joseph and Potiphar's wife was a sober mind. She was led by her desires, and he was led by his convictions. She was more concerned about her needs and wants than she was about her house. In these moments his heart must have been focused on the Lord and not the desires of his flesh.

How often do we find ourselves willing to dishonor both the house we sleep in and the house we worship in? The reality is, we are all capable of finding ourselves unsatisfied in the house or with the plan when we no longer honor the house. Before you risk it all and run off, led by your desires, ask yourself, *Where does God want me?* Remind yourself that God is the One who ultimately placed you there, and then ask yourself why you want to leave. Be careful to go only when God is leading you and only where God is leading you, because we all run the risk of being like Potiphar's wife, dishonoring the house, leaving the people around us to run away naked. Potiphar's wife suddenly lost her control, hoping Joseph would finally give in to her, and she got a little grabby. The Bible tells us she grabbed Joseph's cloak, and when he ran away, he left it in her hands. He most likely had nothing on underneath. That's right, he was probably naked, and he inadvertently gave us what is probably one of the most hilarious runaway scenes in the entire Bible. Joseph wasn't just bolting in minimal clothing. He was taking off from one of the most well-respected houses in Egypt. The sight alone would be a pretty huge scandal. Imagine if you were walking in Washington, DC, and saw a naked man running across the White House's north or south lawn. You wouldn't look at that guy and think, *That right there is a mighty man of character.* You would think, *Golly, someone is streaking at the White House. What bet did he lose?* While it's funny to think about, the truth is that sometimes we are better off *looking* foolish than *acting* foolish.

The Bible says time and time again, "The LORD was with him" or "The LORD was with Joseph" (Genesis 39:2, 3, 21, 23). I believe Joseph was well aware that the Lord was with him, and because he was aware of God's presence and favor in his life, he was faithful to run from sin and follow the Lord's direction.

WHEN THE RIGHT PLACE BECOMES THE WRONG PLACE

Pharaoh's kingdom isn't the only place where some running might be required. There are times in life when, as in Joseph's case, the right house can quickly turn on you, and that would be the right time to run. I'm speaking from my own experience.

I am not just a pastor's kid; I also consider myself a church kid. I wonder how many of you just chuckled because you know what that means. For those of you who don't, let me explain. Church kids are in church *all* the time. All. Week. Long. If the church doors are open, then barring death, major injury, or natural disaster, a church kid can always be found inside the building.

Sometimes I'll go to churches for an event and the pastors will say, "I wish you could have met my son, but he's at a friend's house," or "I really wanted my daughter to meet you, but she had homework." Every time I hear pastors make these statements, I am completely blown away. Like, "You allow your kids not to come to church?" I grew up in a home where nothing came before church—not parties, events, homework, or health, because church was always the best place for me to be.

"You wanna go to an event or a party *instead of* church? You need Jesus. You're coming to church!"

"You're having an issue with your homework? Get to church. God can help you."

"You're not feeling well? *Jesus can heal you.* Put some clothes on and get in the car. We're going to church."

Not going to church was *never* an option.

My parents were the senior pastors of my church, so all my life, no matter what was happening, I was with my family in church almost every night of the week. We spent all day in church on Sunday. On Monday it was singles ministry night. On Tuesday it was marriage ministry night. On Wednesday it was the midweek prayer meeting. On Thursday there were bereavement meetings. On Friday there were senior mixers. I was a church kid.

What I've learned about church kids like me is that we are really easy to spot *outside* of the church. Here's a classic example of what life was like outside of church for me. I was probably eleven years old when I slept over at a friend's house for the first time. Since we live in a small world and I would like to keep this friend, let's rename him. Let's say his name was Satan. One night I stayed over at Satan's house. We were hanging out doing what guys do during sleepovers. We ate pizza, talked sports, didn't get to sleep, and probably "forgot" to shower. It was a typical boys' sleepover. At some point around 3:00 a.m., Satan pulled a dirty magazine out of his backpack. I know! You're all shocked. Maybe even appalled. I promise, I was too.

As he was pulling this magazine out of his bag, every sermon I had ever heard about sexual purity and sexual morality rushed through my mind. When you're a church kid, there's a different level of accountability and fear. The Holy Spirit doesn't just speak to adults. He whispers to eleven-year-olds who are about to look at a dirty magazine! *"Flee from sexual immorality." You have to get out of here, Chris.* But that was easier said than done. I was a chubby white boy with a bowl haircut in the middle of the ghetto. If I tried to leave, I was pretty sure I was going to die on those streets! Then I thought that might actually be cool. I could be the first martyr in the Durso household. I could be the first Stephen of my generation.

I had my parents' permission to be there, but this suddenly became the wrong place for me to be, and this was the right time for me to hightail it out of there. Just as I was about to make a run for it, the phone rang. Satan turned to me and said, "Chris, it's your mom." I pulled myself together and grabbed the phone. With a quick inhale I answered, "Hey, Mom! What's up? We were just praying." It was the middle of the night. I don't know how I thought she would have believed that.

You need to see my mom. She may be petite, but she is powerful. She responded with just four short statements. "So was I. Tell your friend to put down the magazine. I love you. See you in the morning."

Please don't cheer her on, and don't laugh at me. This is my childhood we're talking about! This is how this church kid grew up. I could be in the most remote place on earth, but my mom would know exactly what was going on. This was normal for me. This is what happens to church kids who have a praying mom. She talked to God all day, every day, and apparently all night long too, and He talked back. So as a child I was very careful. I was on guard inside the church and outside of the church. I was hyperaware of what I did, where I went, and who I hung out with. I had a checklist. There were a few important questions on that checklist. *Who am I with? What are they doing? Where are they going? Can this get me into trouble?* I never wanted to be in the wrong place at the wrong time.

My goal was to avoid trouble at all times, to be good, and to make the right choices, especially inside the church, but the truth is there was no escaping outside of church either. I knew the Holy Spirit would rat me out to my mom, and I would be in big trouble. But He didn't speak just to my mom. He would speak to me too, and even though I was only eleven, I knew it. I did not like getting into trouble, so I did my part to avoid it. The Holy Spirit does His job to warn us when it's time to run. We need to know when the right place suddenly becomes the wrong place.

FIGHT OR FLIGHT

One of the guys on Notarbartolo's team was Speedy. He was a longtime friend of Notarbartolo's, but the rest of the team wasn't so sure about him, and they may have had good reason. After the team successfully made it through those layers of security and filled their bags to capacity, carrying an estimated $100 million in diamonds, gold, and jewels, they got into their getaway cars and headed to their meet-up spot in a town not too far away. At some point along the ride, Speedy seemed to have a panic attack. He couldn't wait to get to the meeting place where they would burn all the evidence. He couldn't drive with that garbage in the car, so he tossed the bag of garbage into a wooded area along the side of the highway. Having that bag of evidence in the car stressed him to the point where he had to take action. This was not the plan, but it was too late; the garbage was already flying around.

I would imagine the prodigal son's stress level was just as high as he was preparing to leave his house. His family, his house, his responsibilities were all keeping him from something better. Thinking about that all day and night had to have affected him. Scientists have used the phrase *fight or flight* to describe a physiological response to stress or a threat. When people feel threatened, they have a choice to make: either fight or flee. The son ran; this may have been an instinctive physiological response to what he perceived to be a threat, and for him that threat of an unfulfilled life was inside the house.

I think we can all recall at least one time in our lives when we have either wanted to or had to run, only to find out later that we shouldn't have run.

For me it was my first year of junior high school, before I knew what BO (body odor) was. I was in the middle of a school assembly, and something smelled really bad. It didn't take very long for me to realize that smell was coming from me. *I* smelled. I didn't have the guts to cut school and go back home, because I didn't want to get in trouble, but all day long all I could think about was getting out of there. I wanted to run, and the moment that final bell rang, I ran out of there and went home. I wanted to leave before my friends found out it was me, because this could stick with me for the rest of my junior high years and beyond. This would not be my story.

I later learned that the nurse's office was stocked with deodorant for situations like this. Isn't it ironic how sometimes the very thing you need is already in the place you are running from? The truth is, I didn't know what the solution was, so I couldn't have asked for deodorant if I'd wanted to. When I told my mom about my problem, she laughed. She knew what the solution was the whole time. She went to the pharmacy and bought me my first deodorant. It was a simple solution, but I was so wrapped up in the problem, so consumed with staying below the radar and avoiding my friends, that I didn't ask for help. What could have ended my social life before it even started had a very simple solution, but I was clueless.

How many times have we run, unnecessarily, toward something we thought we needed, or from some perceived threat, because we didn't know what questions to ask or where we could find direction? If we are guided by the Holy Spirit and not by our thoughts, we can avoid going in the wrong direction altogether. I could have avoided one of the toughest days of my junior high experience. We run because we believe we can't be here. That can be true in some instances, but in the case of the prodigal son, he never should have left his home. Running away only delays our getting to the place we hope to reach. His home represented safety, happiness, success, and fortune. He had everything he needed at home, yet something caused him to believe that there was more waiting for him outside of the home and that he had to leave to find it.

ROYAL RUMBLE

There are lots of runners in the Bible, people who are running from God and eventually to God, people who give everything they have to run toward their purpose, and people who run from their purpose with the same ferocity. While Potiphar's wife runs toward sin, Joseph runs to avoid sin, and Jacob runs to avoid the consequences of his sin.

It has to be one of the most dramatic stories in the Old Testament. The story of Jacob, his life and legacy, reads like a tele-novela. Jacob is the son of Isaac, grandson to Abraham (you know, the friend of God). Jacob comes from a line of men who are richly blessed by God, yet he is a hustler, a modern-day scam artist. His name actually *means* "hustler," so we're not completely surprised when we read about Jacob taking advantage of his ailing father, cheating his brother, Esau, out of his birthright, and going on the run.

Isaac knows he is at death's door, and according to Hebrew culture, it is now time to give his firstborn his birthright, his inheritance. Jacob knows what his older brother is about to get, but he wants it for himself. He doesn't forge his father's signature on a will—that would be too easy. Instead his mother gives him the idea to trick his father into thinking Jacob is his older brother, Esau. Jacob apparently believes the inheritance he is entitled to isn't good enough, so Mommy Dearest comes up with the plan: he is to wear his brother's clothes and some animal fur to convince his just-about-blind father that he is Esau, who, by the way, was apparently really hairy, hence the animal fur (see Genesis 27).

Eventually, Jacob gets caught and has to leave his father's camp, which is a nice way of saying he runs away from home. On the run he picks up two wives, and his caravan of family, animals, servants, and possessions grows. When Laban finds out Jacob has been cheating him to get a larger flock of goats, Jacob knows it's time to leave. His father-in-law is a trickster too; he promises Jacob one daughter but gives him a different one. That's how Jacob ends up with two wives. Jacob knows his father-in-law can't be trusted and that things can only escalate. God instructs Jacob to go home to his father's house. He not only sends Jacob back, but He then promises to go with him (see Genesis 29–31).

Near the end of his journey, he has the greatest encounter any man could ever hope or pray for. His possessions and his relationships are set to the side, and it's in this place of isolation where he sees the face of God.

He encounters a man on his journey. They get into a tussle, a wrestling match right there in the middle of the night in the desert. The sun starts to rise, and the man realizes Jacob isn't giving up, so he knocks Jacob's hip out of its socket. While Jacob still hasn't realized whom he's wrestling, he knows this experience is something that would only happen to him once in a lifetime. Whoever this person is that he's wrestling, Jacob wants the man to bless him.

Then the man tells Jacob to let him go, but Jacob is determined to win. Despite the pain he must be feeling, he refuses to let the man go. This wrestling match is the perfect picture of Jacob's life; he seemed to be struggling all his life. He struggled with his brother, he struggled for a blessing, and he struggled for the wife he longed for. But this struggle would be the defining moment for Jacob, so Jacob is determined not to let go. Jacob tells the man he's not going to let him go until he blesses him. The man responds by asking him about his name.

We saw this question posed differently earlier in the story. When Jacob entered his father's tent, we heard Isaac question Jacob about who he was. Jacob claimed to be Esau. Isaac then asked if he was sure and asked for proof. He questioned him three times (see Genesis 27:18, 21, 24). I think it's safe to assume Isaac knew all about Jacob, that he was capable of being an imposter.

Jacob answers the man he is wrestling. This is confession

time, and Jacob doesn't even know it. When he answers "Jacob," he isn't just informing the man of the name that might have been printed on a modern-day birth certificate. He is admitting "I am a hustler, cheater, and liar." It is in that moment that the man blesses him. Who Jacob really was wasn't exactly a secret (see Genesis 32:22–27).

> If we say that we have no sin, we are deceiving ourselves
> and the truth is not in us. If we confess our sins, He is
> faithful and righteous to forgive us our sins and to cleanse
> us from all unrighteousness. (1 John 1:8–9, NASB)

We might be tempted to believe we have to be perfect to have access to a perfect God. We might even think we have to do good to get to God, but God goes to Jacob in the middle of his sin. In this moment when he is alone, fighting and wrestling with God, his confession triggers the unexpected.

What do you do when it's God who is pursuing you, picking the fight with you, and you feel too small to take Him on?

What do you do when you have hit rock bottom, you're all alone, you have nowhere to turn because of the choices you've made, and you've ruined nearly every relationship you've ever had? You fight back. You wrestle. When we press in, go to God, and pray continually, we are not only expressing faith in God, but we're saying we're not going to let go until we hear from

God. When we praise, we wrestle. We are saying that despite what we have done and where we are, God is still God, and He is still worthy of our praise.

The more time I spend wrestling with God, the less fighting I do in my everyday life with my wife, my kids, my finances, my struggles, and my insecurities. Even when we are at our worst, God is capable of giving His best. God is a loving, merciful God who doesn't treat us as our sins deserve. We must only receive Him.

Jacob's story shows us that at our worst, we can be blessed! It's the amazing part of what God came to do when robbing us of our shame. He went through so much to save us, even though we were not necessarily at our most lovable. If Notarbartolo had found a bunch of coal instead of diamonds, do you think for a second he would have just shrugged and taken the coal because of what he knew the coal could become? Not even close. But that is what is so amazing about our God. He loves us at our worst, and He helps us get to our best—as long as we surrender to Him. It feels backward, but when we're dealing with God, surrender leads to a win, not a loss. This is the only wrestling match I know of where everyone is a winner. Jacob won because in his confession he was transformed. God won because He was able to give Jacob a new identity. You win if you're willing to admit who you are and if you're willing to surrender it for something new.

Jacob had been on the run for too long. He had seen and

experienced the face of God. He knew what God looked like—not so much a physical appearance. But when he looked into the face of that man, he encountered the heart of God, the presence of God. He found reconciliation there. There would be no need to continue hustling or running, so he headed home. That's what Jacob really wanted the whole time, and now that he had been face-to-face with God, he could finish that journey home. God longs for our eyes to be fixed on Him so He can prevail in His purpose, His plan, and His will for our lives, and getting to that place may require a little royal rumble.

When You Leave the House, You May End up Stepping into Some Stuff!

The prodigal son leaves home in search of whatever he thinks he is missing and ultimately loses everything as he squanders his inheritance in partying and sleeping around. I wonder how many rounds of drinks he paid for at the local bar, how many people got close to him just so they could get some of what he had.

The Bible tells us there was a famine in the land. When the prodigal runs out of money, can you imagine him asking for a place to stay at the homes of those who had sidled up to him when he was rich? Would the people who were all too happy to be close to him while he had money now be closing their doors on him because his money is gone, he doesn't smell so fresh, and they barely have enough to eat themselves? He learns the hard way how being reckless cost him everything: the friends he had in the house, the friends he made outside the house, his money, his popularity, and now his pride. This son is about to discover what rock bottom really feels like.

When he eventually finds himself hungry and with very limited options, he takes a job working on a farm. With no money to buy himself a meal, he turns to the trough where he likely serves the animals their food. Pigs don't eat fancy food; they eat slop. I am not a farmer, so I have not had firsthand experience seeing or smelling slop, but I can tell you what it is made of. Slop is made by mixing grains and kitchen leftovers: melon rinds, apple cores, the peels of different fruits and vegetables, table leftovers, things people cannot or will not eat. The prodigal son, the man who once had it all, the man who could have had just about any woman he wanted, is now stepping into some stuff to get to the trough to eat kitchen leftovers and the not-so-edible stuff humans would not eat but that pigs can.

I imagine that was not an easy decision to make. To be fair, though, you and I have probably never experienced the kind of hunger that would make us consider, even for a moment, eating the food out of a pig's trough because it is our only option. His biggest mistake wasn't partying or sleeping around. His biggest mistake was thinking this was his only option. He thought he was so far from home and the life he knew that there was no getting out of the mess he found himself in. What's worse than all the sins any one of us could have committed while we were out there, worse than running from God, is thinking there is no turning back or getting out of the mess we've made. The worst kinds of robberies happen when people rob themselves of a happier life because they inaccurately believe their bad decisions already did that.

Chapter 5

THE EXTRA WEIGHT

Letting Go Is Necessary

And then, something happened.
I let go. Lost in oblivion.
Dark and silent and complete.
I found freedom.

—Narrator, *Fight Club*

E xposed secrets have ruined the lives of many celebrities and television personalities. I have often wondered how people go back to a normal life once their darkest secrets have been exposed. Have you ever made the kind of mistake that you wish you could permanently bury? You know, the kind of mistake that would destroy your life, ruin your future, and shame your family if it ever got out?

Sometimes we struggle to receive grace because of our secrets, the dark places in our hearts and lives that we would never want anyone to know about. The closet drinker, the adulterer, the one addicted to pornography—they all suffer silently because the shame they carry serves as a daily reminder that they are not worthy of forgiveness or a fresh start. They can't face their future because they can't confront the truth of their past. They can't forgive themselves. How could anyone else forgive them?

I believe by this point in the parable, the prodigal son is carrying that kind of shame. He has been reduced to eating with the pigs. He had to have been embarrassed. He probably wasn't looking so fresh; he couldn't have smelled very fresh either. I wonder how much guilt and shame affected his every decision as he spiraled his way toward rock bottom. As he walked into the pigpen, he was likely replaying every bad decision he had made up to that point. He probably had on Repeat the sound of every door that was slammed in his face as he asked old friends for help on his way to the trough. He was probably trying to figure out how many people knew how badly he had messed up. Maybe he realized the women he had been partying with were not as attractive or as appealing as he had once thought. As he looked back, that party high wasn't such a great high anymore.

All he had now were his memories, and those memories were suddenly weighing him down: memories of his life before he left his house, the comforts of home, the food, and the warmth and security of a loving family. He was likely wondering how he could have thought life outside of his house would be any better than the life he had inside his house. The weight on his heart and mind was making it impossible for him to think straight or stand up straight.

His heart may have been heavy, but it hadn't been very long ago that his heart was racing and doing backflips as he daydreamed about all the ways he could spend his inheritance. I'm sure he spent plenty of time imagining what he would buy, what he would do, and the people he would do it with. I'm sure once his fortune dried up, all those thoughts were replaced with images of the look in his father's eyes when he had asked for his inheritance. That image was probably seared in his mind. He was probably kicking himself as he realized that if he had only waited, then he wouldn't have broken his father's heart.

Isn't that like Satan, though, to get us to focus on what we might be missing, to lure us into sin or into dangerous or compromising situations by convincing us we cannot live without something? Or he convinces us that God is trying to keep us from something better. The prodigal wanted his father's inheritance, and he wanted it in that moment because he thought he was missing out on something even better.

Isn't that the conversation Satan had in the garden with Eve? He convinced Eve that God was trying to keep them from being more like Him. Listening in on that conversation, we think it seems silly. How could a piece of fruit make anyone all-knowing? But let's not kid ourselves. Isn't that the conversation he has with us all the time, and doesn't it always seem stupid after the deed is done? We think we're smarter, but we entertain those same thoughts and fall into the same trap when our eyes wander and we decide it's okay to explore what we might be missing out on.

Satan's strategies have been the same since the beginning of time, even before the garden. Let's not forget that Satan once went by the name Lucifer, and he was once the most beautiful among all the angels in heaven. His heart became filled with pride, and he somehow convinced one-third of the angels that he was the most magnificent being, even more magnificent than God, and that God was trying to keep them from something. His heart was so full of pride he was thrown out of heaven, and the one-third of angels who bought what he was selling were tossed out of heaven with him (see Luke 10:18; compare Revelation 9:1; 12:7–9). He lives in a place of constant shame, continually trying to make his army bigger than God's. It's a war he is never going to win, so he uses the same old tactics to create as much division as possible and to build an even bigger army of people to spend eternity in hell with him.

Luring us into sin isn't good enough. That's just the beginning. Once he has lured us into sin, he then beats us with shame as we replay every bad decision that brought us into the pigpen in the first place.

I wonder how long it took the prodigal son to realize he had made a serious error. Was it the minute his father looked at him with pain in his eyes and handed over what he had asked for? Maybe he realized he was wrong as he tossed his bag over his shoulder and found himself slouching to the right as he balanced his bag across his back. Maybe it didn't hit him that his life was about to change until he heard the sound of the door slamming shut behind him. Perhaps it wasn't until much later, when he was in the middle of the dance floor with a harem of women dancing around him.

While we may be aware of every bad choice we make while we are making it, we often can't recognize the full weight of our choices until much later. In the case of the prodigal son, I believe he suddenly felt the full weight of his choices and realized he needed to go home in that unbearable moment in the pigpen. When he found himself ankle deep in slop, digging around for a half-eaten apple or a piece of carrot, I imagine he didn't have to bend too low. He realized that even his father's staff was eating better than he was. He was probably already leaning over, now unbalanced and unstable from having carried the weight of the pain he caused his father and the shame he had brought on himself. That was when the prodigal son realized he had hit rock bottom. Regret will often lead us back to what is right.

The first wise decision the prodigal son made was in realizing he needed to go back to the place he never should have left in the first place. He knew he stank, he looked terrible, he was carrying a lot of shame, he failed, he lost it all, he knew his friends were probably going to have a lot to say about what he looked and smelled like, and at this point he probably couldn't deal with his own stench as he came to his senses.

Let's be clear here. There are no degrees of behavior or, more directly, sin. In God's eyes sin is sin, which is why grace is freely given. You and I were never good; we were never good enough to receive what God has for us. He does not move faster to forgive the pastor than he would an adulterer. This logic does not exist in God's economy, and because of our earthly logic, some of us take issue with such equal treatment. When we struggle with God's desire and ability to forgive what we might classify as big sins and small sins and the fact that He forgives all who have fallen short, then we ultimately have an issue with grace. If we can't give grace, then we certainly do not have an understanding of the grace we have been given.

I'm Not as Strong as I Thought

I'll never forget one of my trips to the gym to work out. Confession time: I don't enjoy working out at all. In fact, the only time I somewhat don't mind is when I work out at home. Do you know the difference between working out at home versus exercising in an actual gym? Two words: OTHER PEOPLE!

I love people. I enjoy being around new people and getting to know them. I am an extrovert. I am recharged when I am around people. The only place that isn't true is at the gym. I'll tell you why. On a rare excursion to a local fitness club, I was surprisingly revved up to pump some iron. I grabbed a towel, found the right bench, and took a seat to do some bicep curls. I was ready. Just then, a sweet, mature Asian woman who had to have been in her midsixties approached and asked if I would swap reps with her.

That didn't sound too difficult, so I agreed. Being the gentleman I am, I got up and offered her the first set. She refused, insisting I go first. I did my thing. Gripping the handles with all my might, grunting and breathing hard, I lifted the heavy weights to my shoulders for my first set. It was her turn. I got up, smiled, and stepped aside.

She looked at the weights, looked at me and smiled, and proceeded to add about fifty pounds to the set I had just struggled with. She then did twice as many curls as I had. I felt the heat rise up my neck and to my ears. My cheeks turned a bright red. *What a show-off*, I thought. She smiled again as she got up from the seat and casually motioned that it was my turn. I had to show this geriatric bodybuilder a thing or two about lifting weights. Determined to do as many curls as she had done, I once again took my position, gripped the handlebar, and gave it everything I had. I grunted and pulled, pulled and grunted. Nothing happened. The weight stack would not move. Not an inch. I adjusted my grip, tried harder, with more grunting and deeper breaths, my knuckles turning white as sweat beads streamed down my face. Still nothing. The weight was just too great.

What a fitting illustration of the gospel. The immensity of our carnal nature was so great that Jesus had to bear it on His shoulders, because there was no possible way we could carry it. This is very different than how Notarbartolo handled his loot. There were more jewels than he and his crew could carry out of that vault, so they left a lot of it behind. They just couldn't carry it all. The weight of our mistakes and the weight of our sin has always been too heavy for us to carry, but it's never been too heavy for God. So while Notarbartolo left some of his treasure behind because it was too heavy to carry and while the prodigal son was growing weary and decided to quit running and return home, Jesus takes on the full weight of the cross for you and me.

SHAME IS HEAVIER THAN WE THOUGHT

When Jesus went to the cross, it wasn't for the sinner who was well put together but had made a minor slipup. He didn't bear the shame and agony of the cross, meant for you and me, for the one who occasionally sinned. He endured the cross for all mankind, for all sin, for all eternity. Jesus bore His cross, with the full weight of our sin, because He knew it would be impossible for us to carry it. We carry the consequences, but we could never bear the weight.

The weight of sin is heavier than we realize. I remember one day my wife asked me to move the sofa. She had this idea that the space would open up if we could just move the sofa. We couldn't wait to see our space come together. She painted a gorgeous picture for me. I was so excited about how it would look that I went to move the sofa on my own. I didn't want to wait for someone to help me. I knew the sofa was big and heavy, but we were so excited I had to do it. I walked on over to the sofa with a clear game plan. I went to lift the couch and learned pretty quickly just how heavy this sofa was. I almost threw out my back because I underestimated how heavy it was. I didn't think about the consequences. I just wanted what I wanted.

When we set our eyes on what we want, on the temporary satisfaction this world has to offer or on what is right in front of us, we lose sight of where we are supposed to be and what we're supposed to be doing. We discredit the Enemy and his power to lure us in the wrong direction. We can't really understand the pain and the damage sin causes until we find ourselves in the pigpen, hunched over from the weight of the shame and pain that our sin causes.

While I was reading a biblical text recently, I noticed something that had never before caught my attention: "Pilate was surprised to hear that he [Jesus] was already dead" (Mark 15:44).

Why was Pilate surprised? Did he have higher hopes for Jesus? Why did the news of Jesus's death surprise him? Wasn't he the one who gave the final approval?

I was confused by Pilate's astonishment, so I did some research to help me understand what he was reacting to. As I dug through commentaries, reading the historic facts noted by different theologians and scholars of the Word, I found out that in those days the cross was not necessarily intended to kill people. We might see the cross as a means to death because we know the cross as the place where Jesus ultimately met His death, but that wasn't the original intention of the cross.

The purpose of the cross was to humiliate the very worst criminals. Sending a criminal to the cross was gruesome, so I was surprised to learn that crosses weren't placed in remote areas. The Romans did not host private executions; instead, crosses were out in the open, near busy paths so that everyone could witness them. It was intended to serve as public humiliation. That's why at Jesus's crucifixion we read about soldiers giving him a crown of thorns and shouting, "Hail, King of the Jews!" to mock Him, offering Him sour wine, and "casting lots" for His garments (see Matthew 27; Mark 15; John 19). They pretty much rolled dice to see who would get His clothes. The centurion and his soldiers had done this so many times it wasn't even shocking. They were completely desensitized as they nailed human flesh to a wooden plank. This type of execution was painful.

Criminals on crosses essentially struggled to breathe as the weight of their bodies crushed their lungs and other vital organs, making every single breath incredibly difficult and painful. Men who died on a cross ultimately died from asphyxiation. Criminals who did not die on their crosses could have been taken down at some point and buried alive. Oftentimes the men who actually died on the cross had to be left there for nearly three days.

Jesus's experience, however, was different. Jesus endured the public humiliation, with the full weight of our sin attached to it. He carried His cross, naked. He was then nailed to the cross. His body was lifted onto His stake at Golgotha at 9:00 a.m., and by 3:00 p.m. He was dead. The Bible tells us Jesus died *on the same day* (see Mark 15:25–26, 33–37), only *six hours* later.

How is it that Jesus died so quickly? An average man could endure a few days, but Jesus could only endure a few hours? Was Jesus so weak that He died in record time? Is it possible that the weight of our sin was so heavy it literally took hours, minutes, and seconds off Jesus's life? He wasn't just carrying the weight of the wood; He carried His cross with the weight of our sin attached to it. Let me be clear here. He carried the weight of the sin of humanity—all sin, for all people, for all time. His cross was heavy, yet He freely carried it for us.

Is it reasonable to suggest Jesus died quickly because the weight that was on Him was too heavy? Our sin was not too heavy for Him to handle; He did not have to call for backup. But our sin was so heavy that it ended His life quickly. If it is true that the Son of God died quickly because the weight of our sin was too heavy for His human organs to bear, then how could we, in our mere human state, possibly think we are capable of carrying the weight of our sin? It is a recycled lie planted by Satan himself to draw us away from our purpose and steal the glory he knows full well belongs to God.

My heart's desire is for you to understand that your sin is powerful enough to destroy you and heavy enough to quickly suffocate the life out of you.

God never meant for us to carry around the burden of our sin. He doesn't want to see us hunched over, ankle deep in the consequences of our sin, weighed down by guilt and shame, unable to breathe. When we choose to carry sin, we are cutting our lives short.

I am not suggesting Jesus could not have fought to stay alive. He is God! He absolutely could have, but doing so would have canceled why He took on human form, why He lived among us, why He studied us, and why He plotted the heist in the first place. All His work would have been in vain. The truth is, He actually fought to die. He fought to die so we wouldn't have to fight to figure out how to live with sin. Sin and death do not have to define us; grace does. When we give Him our sin and shame, He gives us His grace. Grace makes it possible for us to live free from the power and weight of sin. God's favor has been given freely to us through His Son, Jesus, who liberates us from sin's power. The reason we feel the heaviness of sin is because we haven't let it go or we have found a way to pick it back up.

We can't handle the weight of sin, and we don't have to. Jesus already carried it. Hand it over.

———

When Notarbartolo was in the vault, at least two levels below the street, he had a decision to make. He and his crew could not carry everything that was in the vault. They had to leave some of it behind. Otherwise the loot would have slowed them down, and they would have risked getting caught. When we insist on carrying the deadweight of our sins, not only are we forced to slow down but we also forfeit our destiny.

We were never supposed to try to carry the weight of our sin. We are only supposed to carry the weight of our purpose. In Psalm 139 King David prays a heartfelt prayer that tells us how long God's eye has been on us. While we were in our mother's wombs, before we saw the light of day, before we decided to sin, before any one of us found ourselves in the pigpen contemplating eating leftover scraps, God knew us and had a master plan in place so we wouldn't have to waste our time digging for scraps.

We were never supposed to carry our sin, because that was Jesus's purpose. He was predestined to bear the full weight of our sin. When we don't let the burden of sin go, when we refuse to receive His forgiveness, we are essentially saying what Jesus did on the cross was not enough.

Luke 9:23 says that if we want to be His disciples, we have to take up our crosses and follow Him. Jesus was not inviting us to carry the cross He carried. We are not sharing in this part of His plan. This isn't an invitation to follow Him to Calvary. Each one of us has a cross we must bear: not the cross of sin but the cross of purpose.

We were never promised an easy road to purpose. Sometimes that road is long and difficult. We will be confronted with the truth of our limitations and our failures. We will be distracted by the everyday challenges of life. We may even be frustrated by the sacrifices we will have to make, but ultimately those challenges and sacrifices will bring us right where we are supposed to be as we continually receive God's grace. We need God's grace to carry out our calling. We need God's grace to be the people God planned for us to be. We need God's grace to do the things He planned for us long before we were even born.

Unlike Jesus, we do not have to be perfect to carry out our purpose. We will make mistakes. We will fall short. We will have moments of discouragement, and we may even make the kinds of decisions that the prodigal son made and find ourselves alone, broke, and digging through trash for something to eat. This doesn't surprise God. It doesn't scare Him away or make Him change His mind about the prodigal son—or us.

I recently watched a video on a social-media platform in which a mother was chasing her third-grade son around a dining room table. She was telling him that he had to be punished for failing a test. Apparently the teacher had called the mother and reported that her son's grades were slipping again. The mother was explaining there had to be consequences, and the son was begging her for mercy. Then he started begging his sister to intervene. When his sister didn't help, he began to pray out loud. When that didn't seem to dissuade his mother, he began to blame God. His mother asked how this was God's fault, and he said, "God made me dumb." Finally, he slapped his own hand. He wanted to punish himself and spare his mother of her need to punish him. His creativity in the negotiation process was impressive, but his need to beg for mercy was heartbreaking.

This interaction was painful to watch because it is exactly what we do when we think we are in trouble with God, when we think we have failed Him. We beg for mercy, we blame Satan for tempting us, we blame God for not making us smart enough or strong enough to avoid the traps, and then we punish ourselves for failing Him.

There is no need to punish ourselves. Imagine Notarbartolo flogging himself if he had been caught in the vault. It would have been laughable. We cannot deliver justice for ourselves. Our human understanding of justice is not the same as the justice of God. When we make mistakes, there are consequences and punishments that legal systems are required to uphold, and those systems and rules are in place to maintain order in communities and nations.

Jesus, however, is the core of a very different justice system. His master plan is unmatched. He is not the mean dean in a boarding school looking to punish all the bad girls and boys. Even when we are at our worst, He is still standing on the sidelines waiting to give us another chance. We see this at the cross. While He is clutching to dear life on one cross, a real criminal is on a cross next to Him. The man asks for forgiveness, and Jesus freely gives it. The criminal does not have to atone for his mistakes. He doesn't have to explain or justify his choices. Yet Jesus freely offers him a place with Him in heaven; he is instantly forgiven the minute he recognizes he needs what Jesus is offering.

> Then he said, "Jesus, remember me when you come into your kingdom."
>
> Jesus answered him, "Truly I tell you, today you will be with me in paradise." (Luke 23:42–43)

If there is one thing Jesus makes clear while He is hanging on that cross, it is this: forgiveness is instant. When the thief next to Him asks for mercy, Jesus instantly gives him mercy by assuring him that he has a place in paradise awaiting him.

While Jesus forgives instantly, we are not so quick to forgive ourselves. Receiving forgiveness can be a challenge for those of us who understand human law; if you commit a crime, you must be punished. Accepting God's master plan requires us to adjust our thinking.

Let me try to help you see this a little more clearly. It's almost like working out. When you want to lose some weight, you implement a workout routine because you know dropping weight will require putting in some work. The same is true about our faith. We need to exercise our faith if we want to lose the weight of our sin. We hear pastors and preachers instructing us to let go of the guilt that weighs us down, but the process isn't as simple as putting our bags on the floor. It's not an instant step. We are instantly forgiven, but letting go requires some time and effort. When we hear and receive this message, we are instantly encouraged, we are instantly inspired, and there is an instant relief in knowing we don't have to carry the weight of our guilt and shame anymore. But the process of actually letting go requires a little working out.

We might be tempted to disqualify ourselves from this. We might have fallen into the trap of thinking we could never receive it because we know exactly what we've done, the sins we carry, the mistakes we've made, the hurt we've caused. Some of us have rap sheets, and we have kept track of every single time we have failed. Meanwhile, Jesus is rooting for us, waiting for us to ask for forgiveness so He can blot out our mistakes from His records.

> Pilate had a notice prepared and fastened to the cross. It read: JESUS OF NAZARETH, THE KING OF THE JEWS. Many of the Jews read this sign, for the place where Jesus was crucified was near the city, and the sign was written in Aramaic, Latin and Greek. (John 19:19–20)

The sign above Jesus's head declaring He was King was written in the three languages of the time and location. While Pilate may have thought he was being facetious, God was ultimately making sure that everyone who walked by Jesus that day would read that sign and know exactly who was up there. This is what a loving father does; he speaks to us in a language we can understand.

I am so grateful we can come to God with anything, even the messy stuff. I am grateful we do not have to carry the shame, the guilt, or the weight of our sin. I am grateful I don't have to try to be perfect, because God knows that, in my humanity, I am limited. Grace tells us that God isn't mad at us no matter how badly we mess up or how far we run from where we are supposed to be. Grace makes it possible for me to stop running. Grace makes it possible for you to go home again. What's even better is that we don't have to wash up before we get there. We don't have to prepare an elaborate speech or apology. Grace makes it possible for us to turn around and go back to where we are supposed to be. Grace makes it possible for God to come to me even as I turn back to Him, still covered in sin.

Chapter 6

THE COMEBACK

Home Is Always an Option

I'm gonna make him an offer
he can't refuse.

—Don Vito Corleone (Marlon Brando),
The Godfather

S ometimes instead of moving forward, we end up going back to old places, places we once hated. We believe the lie that this is the one thing God was trying to keep us from.

There will always be people who never take advantage of the fact they can go home again because they simply won't receive grace. There are also plenty of people who accept that God will forgive them, so they happily receive grace for themselves, but they cannot extend the same grace and courtesy to anyone else. Let's examine the scenario just before Jesus's death. It's Passover, and Jesus instructs the disciples to get dinner together. The disciples gather around the dinner table as they had done before, except just as they are breaking bread—in essence Jesus is distributing the first communion—Jesus announces someone at that table will betray Him.

At this table the disciples are breaking bread with their closest brothers in the faith. The cheerful energy is probably sucked right out of the room as Jesus announces that someone in the inner circle is about to betray Him. This is a brother in the faith He is talking about. How could this be?

With the very coins he had been paid to betray Jesus sitting in his pocket, Judas doesn't confess, nor does he ask for forgiveness when Jesus announces that someone at that table will betray Him. Instead, Judas leaves the dinner party without saying a word. Have you ever wondered what kind of response Jesus would have had if Judas had confessed when Jesus gave him the chance? Given how Jesus handled the lepers, the adulterers, and the tax collectors He encountered and His posture when He reclined at the table, I believe Judas would have found forgiveness there. Unfortunately, Judas doesn't know how to ask for forgiveness, or he simply doesn't believe he deserves forgiveness. Instead, Matthew 27 tells us that once Judas learns that Jesus will be crucified, Judas doles out his own punishment on himself. He returns the silver pieces he made betraying Jesus and then hangs himself. It's a shame Judas didn't realize that Jesus was capable of forgiving him.

⁓

Interestingly enough, back in Luke 15, once the prodigal son realizes he has hit rock bottom, he finally comes to his senses and decides he is going back home. This is the first wise decision the prodigal son makes. While he is burdened by the weight of his actions, he realizes he *needs* to go back home, back to the place he never should have left. He goes back home, just as he is, stinking like a pig and all.

I wonder how many times during that long walk home he stopped to consider what his friends or family might say of him in his current condition. I bet the smell that came from his filthy clothes continually reminded him of just how dirty he was. That's what guilt will do to us. Our mistakes will tell us we can't go home.

I bet he also struggled with hunger pangs; the longing for the meals he once enjoyed didn't escape him either. Torn between his shame and his desire for the comforts of home, he somehow finds the courage to keep walking. He knows he has to go back home. I bet that was a journey he wouldn't soon forget.

How many speeches do you think the son wrote as he walked back home? The story tells us he planned to get up, return to his father, and start with an apology: "I have sinned against heaven and before you" (Luke 15:18, esv). How many versions of that apology did he come up with before he landed on opening with a confession? He must have planned when he would say it and how he would say it. It had to be convincing. He must have known how badly he had hurt his father. I'm sure he struggled to find the right combination of words, but what are the right words when you know you have failed so miserably, broken your father's heart, embarrassed yourself, and are now walking back home with nothing but dirty laundry?

> For all have sinned and fall short of the glory of God, and all are justified freely by his grace through the redemption that came by Christ Jesus. (Romans 3:23–24)

Some time ago my son, Dylan, asked me if he could stay up late to watch television. I reminded him it was a school night, and I sent him off to bed. In the middle of the night, I woke up to the sound of the TV coming from his room. I walked in and found him lying on his bed, arms behind his head watching the television with both the air conditioner and a fan on. I said, "DYLAN! I thought I told you to go to sleep!" He immediately jumped out of his bed and fell on the floor in front of me, crying. With tears streaming down his face, he started confessing how he had failed me; he started begging for forgiveness. While this was dramatic, I saw his heart. He was really sorry. I picked him up, wiped his tears, and kissed him on the head.

As he heard and sensed me forgiving him, as he experienced forgiveness, he almost immediately started smiling. He has a greater understanding of forgiveness than most seasoned Christians. He understood that the moment he apologized, he was forgiven. He didn't have to walk around sad for days or weeks until he was done punishing himself. He released himself of all guilt and shame. He gave himself permission to enjoy the gift I was offering. We could all learn from my son how to receive a pardon.

There's nothing spiritual about walking around like a depressed cartoon character with a storm cloud hovering overhead. The greatest lie we believe is that we have to atone for our mistakes. We have to know that when we are forgiven, we are free from sin as well as its shame and guilt. We have to receive that forgiveness and move on with the joy of the Lord.

I have to be honest, though; moving with the joy of the Lord isn't always easy. I imagine it would have been nearly impossible for a man like Hosea to take Gomer as his wife. We read about them in the Old Testament in the book of Hosea. Hosea was a prophet, and Gomer was a prostitute. God had given Hosea instructions not only to marry Gomer but also to have children with her. Hosea was obedient, but at some point after they had children, Gomer left Hosea and returned to her job on the streets.

Poor Hosea. He was obedient, but can you imagine the shame he felt as his family and neighbors began to notice his wife was missing? They hadn't been invited to a funeral, so where could she have gone? But Hosea knew where she was. She had returned to her old lifestyle, worshiping false gods and making money on her back. Hosea didn't have to figure out what to do next, because God gave him instructions: go get her and love her with the love of the Lord.

God didn't want Hosea to sit around waiting for her. He was sending Hosea to rescue her, and again, out of obedience, Hosea did as the Lord asked even though it could have meant catching her in the act. If you can imagine being in Gomer's shoes, imagine what that must have been like as your husband walked in and asked how much it would cost to buy you back. What about the moments following? What was that journey home like? Was there an apology? Did Gomer even want to go back home? It's not as if she had been kidnapped. This was a decision a grown woman had consciously made.

What does a prostitute look like, smell like, and feel like after a long day or a long week? She had been carrying a piece of every man she had been with. There was no way to lighten the heavy burden she had been carrying. The guilt that must have been sitting on her chest at night when she finally lay down to sleep had to make it difficult to do so, and no bath would help her escape the stench of her sin.

> The LORD said to me, "Go, show your love to your wife again, though she is loved by another man and is an adulteress. Love her as the LORD loves the Israelites, though they turn to other gods and love the sacred raisin cakes."
>
> So I bought her for fifteen shekels of silver and about a homer and a lethek of barley. Then I told her, "You are

to live with me many days; you must not be a prostitute
or be intimate with any man, and I will behave the same
way toward you." (Hosea 3:1–3)

While she was out doing her own thing, God sent Hosea to
get her back. Not only did Hosea buy back what was already his,
but he was also instructed to treat his wife with love and kindness. That's not how a typical man would respond. He would
fight God, demand justice, and make her pay. She would know
exactly how he felt about her. But God doesn't do that. God goes
after her with grace in an effort to restore her.

She probably couldn't even look at her husband. Her shame
probably caused her to hang her head low, but if Hosea was obedient, then he probably couldn't keep his eyes off her. Have you
ever expected to be in trouble but instead were met with love and
compassion? Can you imagine how this would have made her
feel? Encounters with grace take a lot of getting used to because
it's like nothing we've ever experienced before; it is pure, with no
ulterior motive.

To be rescued is one thing, but then to be treated like royalty
is another. God didn't just save you to save you. He saved you so
that He can love you.

O Israel, come back! Return to your GOD!
   You're down but you're not out.

Prepare your confession
    and come back to GOD.
Pray to him, "Take away our sin,
    accept our confession.
Receive as restitution
    our repentant prayers." (Hosea 14:1–2, MSG)

Hosea's actions prove that it is possible for us to love as Jesus loves (the 1 Corinthians 13 way), no matter what anyone says or does to us. Hosea and Gomer further prove that Judas could have gone home. He didn't have to go to that tree because of the heist Jesus was about to pull off.

Given the audience and the players Jesus puts in the scene as He is telling the parables found in Luke 15, I believe He was trying to show us a full picture of the gospel and giving an open invitation for all to receive grace. Is it possible we have forgotten that we don't have to have it all together and that we all need what He is offering?

At the risk of raising some eyebrows, I might suggest the parable of the prodigal son needs to be renamed. "The Prodigal Son" implies that this story of grace and restoration is solely about a young, rebellious son who wanders off. But these grace stories suggest that grace is just as much for the one who stays and does the right thing as it is for the one who runs off and makes all the wrong choices. Every single one of us needs a revelation of grace at different times in our lives. Jesus was saying . . .

When your heart is lonely and longing for more, you can come to Me.

When you're tired of failing, you can come to Me.

When you've come up empty handed, you can come to Me.

When you're dirty and you reek of sin, you can come to Me.

If you've become religious, come to Me.

If you've been faithful but you're frustrated and have lost hope, come to Me.

> Are you tired? Worn out? Burned out on religion? Come to me. Get away with me and you'll recover your life. I'll show you how to take a real rest. Walk with me and work with me—watch how I do it. Learn the unforced rhythms of grace. I won't lay anything heavy or ill-fitting on you. Keep company with me and you'll learn to live freely and lightly. (Matthew 11:28–30, MSG)

We've all had "Judas" moments, moments when we have to decide to repent or not. How we respond in those moments could change the trajectory of our lives; we don't have to have a "Judas" outcome. Judas didn't need to hang himself from a tree because Jesus was about to hang Himself from a cross. His story might have ended differently if he had only stuck around until

Sunday, Easter morning, when the sting of death and the shame of sin were robbed in an instant. Judas didn't think he could go back to his crew because, in his head, what he had done was unforgivable, but Jesus was about to take on the burden of the unforgivable, and Judas missed out.

When we examine Judas's story, we see that Jesus wants to invade Judas's reality, but Satan wants Judas to stay trapped in Judas's version of reality. Judas's betrayal is a moment of weakness, but this is no different from any moments of weakness we have had during our lifetimes, faced with the truth of our sin and debating how to handle it. We are closer to Judas than we think. Any one of us could slip away and choose not to ask for forgiveness. Jesus would have dealt with him the same way Jesus later dealt with Peter's denials and how He later handled Thomas's doubts that he was standing in front of the resurrected Jesus. In His infinite mercy, oftentimes God will give us more than one chance to make our relationships right with Him and to bring our hearts into alignment with His.

What makes the gospel so great is that it removes our debts and then lavishes us with prosperity as if we actually deserve it. Of course we can go back home. Judas was too afraid to go home, but he *could* have gone home. Gomer might have been dragged back home, but she went home and was met with unexpected, undeserved love and kindness.

At some point every single one of us needs a fresh outpouring of grace. It's freely given. We need grace to pick ourselves up and dust ourselves off when we trip. We need grace to help us turn back to where we're supposed to be when we've wandered off, and we need grace to walk out our purpose.

Satan would have us believe we can't go back home. He is quick to remind us of our sins, of our mistakes, of our shortcomings, but none of that matters, because when Adam and Eve messed up, grace was already moving toward them, ready to cover them before they even said a word.

Chapter 7

THE BIG MOMENT

When It All Goes Down

The thief comes only in order to
steal and kill and destroy. I came
that they may have and enjoy life,
and have it in abundance (to the
full, till it overflows).

—John 10:10, AMPC

Has anyone ever told you, "There are just some things in life that you have to do on your own"? It might be nice to have some help with those upcoming SAT tests or the bar exam. It would be great if you could have someone handle the math part of the test or the essay section, but no one is going to take you seriously in college or hire you as a lawyer if you can't pass those tests on your own. What about your driving test? Parallel parking is stressful when you are used to pulling right into your driveway, but the Department of Motor Vehicles would not approve of your having someone else come in and do that for you. There are certain things we just have to do for ourselves.

I remember that incredible day when I proposed to my wife. I was a little nervous. I wanted to say the right thing. I wanted every moment to be perfect, but I couldn't exactly hire someone to propose for me. I know that sounds ridiculous, but I am dragging this out for a reason. There are things that only you can do. An understudy, a stand-in, a substitute will not do when you are born to do something.

It would do us well to fully understand that the God we serve requires us to do some things on our own. In other words, no one can do the right thing for you, no one can repent for you, no one can respond to God for you, no one else can proclaim what God has done in you and for you, no one can worship for you, no one can praise Jesus for you, and no one can see the glory of God for you.

What about your cross: Is it possible for someone to carry out your purpose for you?

> Whoever wants to be my disciple must deny themselves
> and take up their cross daily and follow me. (Luke 9:23)

In this verse Jesus is giving the disciples "the clause." He always seemed to start with the end in mind. Jesus was explaining that we each have a cross to carry. He was foretelling His own cross and warning the disciples that following Him would not be easy, that following Him would require sacrifice, and He was making it clear that every single one of them would have his own cross of purpose to carry.

After Jesus was flogged and abused, while He was walking up the hill of Golgotha to be crucified, we meet a man named Simon. He's referred to as Simon of Cyrene. The Bible describes Jesus as being in so much physical agony that it was hard for

Him to walk up this hill while carrying the cross. So they forced Simon of Cyrene to help Him carry the cross (see Mark 15:21–22). In this moment there is so much symbolism and foreshadowing taking place, but before we go there, let's just focus on the simple fact that Jesus had help carrying His cross.

We might be tempted to find a Simon to help us carry our cross. Looking for someone to whom we can delegate the burden and responsibility of our own cross might be tempting, but it won't work. Our cross is our cross. No one else can live out our purpose for us!

This might seem scary, but be encouraged. We have not been left to figure this out on our own. It would be unimaginable for a Father to move heaven and earth in order for His children to know Him, to give everything He has, including sacrificing His Son, only to leave His children to their own devices, to abandon them, to hope they can figure out their existence on their own. If God gives us a plan, we have to trust He is going to show us how to walk it out.

The prodigal son didn't just lose sight of what he had at home; he lost sight of his purpose, the plan God had designed just for him. His eyes wandered onto what was potentially awaiting him beyond what he had at home, and it caused him great heartache.

We are predestined "to do good works" (Ephesians 2:10),

but it would be very difficult for God's plan to come to fruition if we ran in the opposite direction of where we need to be or should be.

God's grace strengthened Jesus as He sat in the garden praying and preparing to carry His cross. God's grace is also available to us; it enables and strengthens us to carry the cross that God has given each one of us. Deuteronomy 31:8 tells us, "The LORD himself goes before you and will be with you; he will never leave you nor forsake you. Do not be afraid; do not be discouraged." This isn't an outdated Old Testament promise; it's a promise you and I can carry in our hearts. He doesn't just send us off to fulfill our purpose by ourselves; He goes with us!

I'm the youngest of three. When we were kids, I was my brothers' personal butler. My brothers were bigger. If they wanted me to do something, I usually had no choice but to do it. I remember my brothers sending me downstairs to the kitchen to get them a drink in the middle of the night. It was dark, and I was scared, so I would ask, "Can you come with me?" Their response was always the same. "No! If I wanted to go downstairs, I would have gone myself." My request for them to come with me was pretty ridiculous.

Aren't you glad my brothers aren't the ones sending us? They'd make us pursue our purposes alone. The King of kings, however, promises to go with us. He wants to walk with you. He says you don't have to do it alone.

He created the universe! He responds to the needs and requests of every human being. He is mindful of every living thing, but He still promises to go with us. God's assurance to go with us isn't only about our not being alone; His assurance tells us that our purpose is important to God and that with Him on our side, we cannot fail.

Our purpose, our calling, may be scary, but we have to know we were built for our calling. In the same way Jesus had everything He needed to fulfill His calling, you and I have everything we need to fulfill our calling—not just a part of it, but the whole thing.

When my wife and I serve our kids dinner, we sometimes get the question every parent cringes to hear: "Do I have to eat all of it?" I love my kids, but that question baffles me every single time. Why would I serve him more than he could handle? Why would I give her more than what she needs? If your Father put something on your plate, you can handle it. All of us have been given a plate, and our portions have been predetermined. If you're looking at only your plate, you see a fragmented picture. You're going to see what has been asked of you and miss the fact that the One who has called you is right in front of you, ready to give you whatever you need to carry your cross. I know it may sometimes seem like too much, but you were built for this!

I wonder how many of you are looking at the assignment on your plate and are wondering if you've been given a plate where all the letters have been scrambled. I don't believe God served you alphabet soup. Let today be the day you stop questioning what's on your plate. Pastor. Worship leader. Business leader. Missionary. Community leader. Hope-giver. Spouse. Parent. Son. Daughter. Friend. You are called, set apart, and predestined to change the status quo wherever you are.

BUSTED

When a thief is caught red-handed, the consequences and the penalty can be severe, but what about when the mastermind gets caught before he actually pulls off his heist? Is the punishment the same or less severe?

Jesus was turned in by one of His own friends, one of His partners, Judas. Jesus was arrested, tried, and sentenced to death before He actually pulled off His heist. With no evidence and only hearsay, Jesus was publicly paraded around town and sent to His death. Along the way He had some trouble carrying His cross; He stumbled a few times. That's when they pulled someone from the crowd, Simon of Cyrene, and had him carry Jesus's cross. Simon is described as an innocent bystander. Some translations say he was a "passer-by" or was "passing by" (Mark 15:21). He was just trying to get from point A to point B, but as he was doing so, there was a roadblock, which was the Roman guards walking Jesus up the hill to be crucified. Simon is now introduced into the narrative. We go from never having heard of the guy to his getting a big role on a massive day. Think about this day. This had to be the worst day in history, but at the same time it was the greatest day in history. It was the worst day because it was the day that man decided to kill God, but it was the greatest day because it was the day that God decided to kill death. And yet for Simon it had probably been just a normal day, but not anymore. He was thrown into the situation, and he was made to carry this cross. Can you imagine what was going through his mind as he carried this cross? We don't know if he was in shape or how strong he actually was. In fact, we have no idea why he was picked to get involved in a situation that had nothing to do with him—BUT THAT'S JUST IT. It had everything to do with him. In this moment we get a glimpse of what life would have looked like if we were made to carry the cross that Jesus carried, which was OUR CROSS OF SIN.

Although it was our cross of sin, it was Jesus's cross of purpose. I'm sure Jesus could have carried the cross up the hill without the help of Simon, but I believe He wanted to give us an illustration of what was actually going to happen.

The Bible says that Simon helped Jesus carry His cross, but the truth is, Jesus also helped Simon. That wasn't Jesus's cross; that was Simon's cross. Jesus never sinned. He was the spotless lamb. Simon should have carried that cross all the way up the hill. He should have been nailed to it. He should have hung from it. It should have been his blood. We don't know much about him, but he represents humanity. He was a sinner just like the rest of us.

When Simon walked with Jesus to His death, it was so he could escape his own death. Jesus actually carried Simon's cross. That cross belonged to Simon and the Roman centurion who put Him up there; it belonged to Pilate and Barabbas; it belonged to thief number one and to thief number two. The cross belonged to Judas and every murderer, adulterer, idolater, liar, and thief across all time. That cross belonged to both you and me!

Simon was no innocent bystander. There were no innocent bystanders or random people who got caught up in the execution of an innocent man. We are all responsible for Jesus's death. We are all responsible for that cross. Everyone who has walked this earth is responsible, except for the one man who actually carried it—Jesus.

It was at the top of Golgotha that a great exchange was made. When Jesus took the cross from Simon and died in his place, the gospel was fulfilled, and the greatest heist of all time was committed. Jesus stole Simon's spot.

If I could put a meme in this book, it would have a picture of Jesus, and across the bottom it would say, "I got it from here! You should be up on this cross right now, but I got it from here!"

Because of the work Jesus did on that hill, we don't have to make the distinction between the "good" son and the "bad" son. On that hill He took all sin. On that hill He took your death and mine. On that hill He took our guilt and shame. What was lawfully meant for us was taken by Jesus. Our cross of sin was Jesus's cross of purpose. Jesus made that exchange to fulfill His mission on earth; He came to give us a John 10:10 life. He wanted us to have life abundantly.

> The thief comes only in order to steal and kill and
> destroy. I came that they may have and enjoy life, and
> have it in abundance (to the full, till it overflows). (John
> 10:10, AMPC)

In His perfect plan, the Mastermind never intended for us to carry the weight of our sin. That was Jesus's job. We are only supposed to carry the weight of our purpose. The weight of our sin is shame, and it weighs us down. We cannot operate from a place of shame. We cannot carry out our purpose while we are carrying our sin and shame. The prodigal son could not fulfill his purpose while he was filthy with sin and shame. He had to release his shame in order to go back to where he was supposed to be. You have to let them go!

The first time you repented was enough, whether it was at an altar call or you were alone in your room. At that moment Jesus took on your sin so you could take on your purpose.

All the evidence was submitted against Jesus years ago. An innocent man was found guilty, and He was given His cross. The only problem is they executed the wrong man. He willingly carried that cross because His eye was on the prize. *You* are the prize. His sacrifice allows you to give Him your garbage.

Imagine someone breaking into your house, bypassing the fifty-inch flat-screen television, the latest smartwatch, and the diamond bracelet your grandmother left you, and stealing only the trash from your kitchen and your bathroom. Imagine him stopping to wash your dirty dishes and do a few loads of laundry before he leaves. It's unthinkable. Yet that is exactly what Jesus did. As He took that cross back from Simon, He swapped places with all humanity. He stole our shame, our guilt, and our trash, and in exchange we receive life abundantly as we live out our purpose. And if that wasn't enough, we also get a personal invitation to the celebration that will happen in heaven when He calls us home.

One time my wife, Yahris, and I were traveling out of the country for ministry. Traveling is never easy for our family, especially when Yahris and I are leaving the country. We have to plan for every possible scenario; we have to find the right babysitter and make sure we're not gone too long, which is why we don't do it too often. Needless to say, tensions were high. There was so much to coordinate and communicate. My wife doesn't travel well; long flights take a lot out of her. Add to that the logistics of planning such an expedition, and we have the makings of a stressful trip.

I remember boarding that plane, praying that God would upgrade Yahris so she could enjoy her flight and get some much-needed rest. The seats we had were both middle seats in the back of the plane. I guess I did some "good praying" that day, because just minutes before we took off, this older gentleman, accompanied by a flight attendant, began walking straight toward us. He offered to trade his first-class seat in exchange for one of our seats so he could sit in the back with the rest of his family. He earned the better seat. It was his. We were in our rightful seats, but he still wanted to make the trade.

That is a picture of grace. In our lives God comes to where we are and says, "Let's switch seats. You take what you don't deserve, and I'll take what you were given." He knows that without His grace we cannot travel well, that this life is too hard with the everyday challenges and the weight of our sin and shame. He knows we can't make it very far sitting in the seat we deserve.

You and I should have been dragged away in handcuffs that day at Calvary. We deserved the punishment Jesus received. He stole our penalty right out from under us, and it's not a secret. We wouldn't be the only ones to have deserved death that day. Remember Barabbas? He was a real criminal, and because Jesus had to die that day, he got to walk away from his own certain death.

The gospels of Matthew, Mark, and Luke record Jesus being taken to Pilate. It was during Passover, and according to custom, a Passover tradition would allow one criminal to be released. The crowds would decide who would go free. As Pilate presented the options to release a known criminal or the One he would call the King of the Jews, the crowds chose Barabbas. It must have been agonizing for Jesus to hear them cheer, "Give us Barabbas!" Jesus switched seats with Barabbas, who got the upgrade to first class and didn't even know it.

The prodigal son is about to switch seats too. As his father sees him in the distance, he takes off to meet his son. The moment he embraces his son, he robs his sinful son of the consequences of his choices. He takes his garbage and his mess, and he restores him to the family table.

Grace and justice are at constant odds with each other. Justice required the earth be flooded and nearly all humanity wiped away. Grace found Noah and required an ark be built to save a remnant of humanity. Justice would demand the younger brother be banished from the house. Grace gives the son an open invitation to a party in his honor. Justice demands we sit in the back of the airplane and get what we paid for. Grace gives us an upgrade to a seat we could never afford.

That's why you and I get another chance to live out our purposes. Justice would demand our banishment from God's presence. Grace gives us access to the full glory of God. Satan would have us believe otherwise. Let's look one more time at how the parable of the prodigal son starts in Luke 15.

Verse 11 starts in the middle of the scene with just two words: "Jesus continued." What exactly was He continuing? Back up to verse 1, and you will find He shared two more stories before He talked about the prodigal son. Those two parables were about recouping something that was lost. This was a re-peated theme. Jesus was sending us a message. He doesn't give up on the lost; He goes out of His way for the lost, and there should be great celebration when the lost are found and return home.

IT IS NEVER TOO LATE

In an interview Leonardo Notarbartolo explained how he got started in his life of crime. When he was six years old, his mother sent him to buy some milk. He discovered the milkman sleeping and took advantage of the opportunity to steal his money. He got caught, but he said that he knew at that moment that this would be his purpose in life. In an interview in 2003, he said he was born to be a thief, and that is exactly what he did. He lived a life of crime, robbing people and businesses for more than thirty years. Released from prison on parole in 2009, it is not too late for him either. Despite his many run-ins with the law and the life of crime he has chosen, he can still turn his life around. He could decide to use his talents to help businesses improve their security systems to prevent another diamond heist. The choice is his.

How many of you are thinking it is too late to be reinstated in your assignment? In the story of the prodigal son, he decided to go home to ask for a job. He wasn't expecting to be reinstated as a son; he was hoping to be hired as part of the help.

Isn't that just like Satan, though? He convinces us that we are too far away from where we're supposed to be, that too much time has passed, that our sin is too ugly and our shame is too great to be reinstated into the family.

We are sons and daughters, and as such we should never expect crumbs from a table that has place settings with our names on them, ready for us to return.

Luke 15:10 alludes to the idea that heaven wants reasons to celebrate. Jesus says, "I tell you, there is rejoicing in the presence of the angels of God over one sinner who repents."

It would not be too hard to find someone who will accuse you or remind you of your sin. Your enemies will accuse you. Church folk will accuse you too. Those closest to you will accuse you. But here's the real heist: the prodigal son is not punished for wandering off. For the one who is feeling lost, know that your Father has already planned the party and that He is running toward you to cover you with righteous robes. Robes you could never earn on your own. Robes He doesn't expect you to earn. The older brother was self-centered and didn't seem to have any compassion, considering what his brother must have gone through, but he isn't dealt with harshly either. Instead, the father goes outside to meet him too and reassures him that all that the father has is also his (see verse 31). Everything both sons need is already in the house. The father invites the older brother in to celebrate his brother's new life, just as the angels celebrate. The father doesn't cry over the lost time; instead, he chooses to celebrate the return.

God isn't waiting for you to finish punishing yourself before He restores you. He doesn't need you to beg Him either. Your dirt and stains don't intimidate Him. He isn't afraid of your stench. He isn't worried about what the neighbors will say. He is prepared to cover your sin and set your feet on a new path. He is willing to take your trash because He is longing for your worship.

He invites us into the celebration so we can brag on Him. When He brings us into the celebration, He gets to brag about what He did. When we share our testimonies, when we tell people what Jesus did for us, when we are shining the light on Jesus, we get to brag, and ultimately we give to the Father, the One who deserves all our worship, all the glory.

Chapter 8

THE GETAWAY

Grace Is the Vehicle

Anybody can get the goods.
The hard part's getting away. . . .
You plan a good enough getaway,
you could steal Ebbets Field.

—Joe Moore (Gene Hackman),
The Heist

When we last checked in with Leonardo Notarbartolo, he had collaborated with some of the best security guys and locksmiths around, and together they planned the ultimate heist. They were each about to have an awesome payday. Notarbartolo had a great plan. He worked his way through tight security. His team managed to go undetected by the twenty-four-hour guards who patrolled the three-block radius and the cameras that tracked every moment down every street and through every corridor. They had a replica of the vault built and practiced every move. They thought through every possible scenario, except for garbage and panic attacks.

One of the guys on his team, Speedy, began to panic as they drove away from Antwerp. They were supposed to get rid of all the evidence and their DNA, but Speedy panicked and made a mess of things. His job was to take any evidence that could link them to this heist (unfinished food, gloves, maps, keys, and so on) and set it on fire in an empty ditch. Apparently he rushed and did not set the trash on fire. The owner of the lot called the police when he discovered someone had dumped trash on his property, and in just a matter of days, the evidence pointed to Notarbartolo, and he was caught.

God, on the other hand, had a perfect plan from the very beginning. He had grace ready before we even knew we needed it, and unlike Notarbartolo, His success was not contingent on anyone else executing the plan. What Jesus was about to do was not done under the cover of night with no witnesses; it was done in the morning for everyone to witness, and He didn't have to depend on other people to do their part. This was all on Jesus.

This Mastermind had a plan that included covering the prodigal in his sin and welcoming him back home at his worst. A plan that included the older brother, the religious one who seemed to be doing the right thing on the outside but was clearly bothered by the mistakes of the one who wasn't as wise on the inside. A plan that put Jesus, the most righteous and holy of thieves, who took our shame, our sorrow, on a wooden cross, with the weight of our sin and shame nailed up there with Him so the Father could welcome us home.

When my wife and I found out we were having our first child, we began preparing for his arrival. There were lots of decisions we would have to make; there were months of planning and weeks of preparation. Would he sleep in our bed, in his own crib, in his own room? We navigated those months well. We had it together. Then the ninth month rolled around, and Yahris started having Braxton-Hicks contractions, the practice contractions a woman feels before the baby is actually ready. About that time something changed; a new level of reality set in. We knew the clock was winding down and our son would be with us soon. There was a different sense of urgency as the last month turned into the final weeks and days. This was really happening; we were about to see the boy we'd prayed for, planned for, and watched kick from inside my beautiful wife's belly.

Jesus had been talking about the coming kingdom. He and the disciples had discussed it at length. They knew everything was going to change, but they didn't sense the urgency until John was arrested (see Matthew 4:12). When the prophecies of Isaiah began to come to fruition, Jesus knew the end was close. From that moment forward Jesus turned up the narrative: "The kingdom of heaven is at hand" (Matthew 4:17, ESV). The disciples were anticipating heaven, but heaven was already there, walking and talking with them. When Jesus is present, heaven is already present.

As Jesus walked through the city streets, He had one message, and it was an open invitation to follow Him. This was the shortest message and the shortest lesson He had taught. The longest message is in the next chapter. In Matthew 5 we have what are now referred to as the Beatitudes.

The word *beatitude* means "supreme blessedness." Jesus, the greatest preacher ever to walk the earth, was about to deliver one of the greatest messages ever given on humility. Jesus was a master communicator as He had built-in illustrations. Expert communicators will tell you to use a visual aid when you are preaching because visual cues always make it easier for people to remember the message.

Jesus took full advantage of His abilities. He made the oceans and the land. Then He walked on the water and told the disciples to walk by faith. In the story where He wants the people to know that God can do anything, they believe He can. Their faith can multiply anything, including loaves and fish.

After the people had seen what Jesus had done, they joined the disciples in following Him, people by the thousands. In their minds this guy was it. He was the one to follow. He said revolutionary things. He had a different aura about Him. He was magnetic, and He was on top.

The rabbis were trying to bash Him. He did things very differently, so they could not understand why people wanted to follow Him around. He was a popular preacher. He walked up a mountain and then sat down. We're going to slow this down so we don't miss anything in this event. Visually, Jesus was standing on top of a mountain, but He had no problem getting low. There were messages pointing toward this in everything He said and did.

His teaching style was direct but not abrupt. He taught the disciples everything they need to know without actually spelling it all out for them every time. Have you ever tried to tell somebody something without actually saying the words you mean? Everyone knows at least one person whose breath isn't exactly fresh. Instead of telling him that his breath stinks, you start digging around in your backpack for a piece of gum, telling him you are really craving a piece of gum and secretly hoping the guy with the bad breath wants gum too.

Jesus was strategic. While He was teaching the disciples, He was also aware that the people following Him were listening and that they would get it too.

In Matthew 5:3 we don't just see a nice statement; this is an exclamation, an attention-getter: "Blessed are the poor in spirit." When I think about great opening lines, I am not sure this statement is it. The Hebrew word for "poor" is a word picture that actually means someone is on the ground. While He sat on the ground on the top of this mountain, He was saying, "Blessed are those who are on the ground, begging for more of God." There's a difference between asking and begging. Begging communicates desperation, desperation from knowing that you don't have it, that you need it, and that you'll do whatever it takes to get it.

In verse 4 He continued, "Blessed are those who mourn." This is an odd group of people to speak a blessing over. Is Jesus saying that if I want to be blessed, I have to look up the obituaries to find people who are mourning so I can mourn with them? No, that's not what He is saying, but when we are *desperate* for a blessing, we'll do whatever it takes to get our blessing. Fortunately, we do not have to go looking for a family that is grieving, because this verse is about someone who is willing to die.

Every day you need to wake up to your own funeral. It's not about harping on your testimony but instead being grateful while mourning the person you once were. When you mourn, you recognize who you were, and you become increasingly grateful for new mercies.

In the following verses He speaks blessings over specific groups of people:

> Blessed are the meek,
>> for they will inherit the earth.
>
> Blessed are those who hunger and thirst for
>> righteousness,
>
>> for they will be filled.
>
> Blessed are the merciful,
>> for they will be shown mercy.
>
> Blessed are the pure in heart,
>> for they will see God.
>
> Blessed are the peacemakers,
>> for they will be called children of God.
>
> Blessed are those who are persecuted because of
>> righteousness,
>
>> for theirs is the kingdom of heaven.

Blessed are you when people insult you, persecute
you and falsely say all kinds of evil against you because
of me. Rejoice and be glad, because great is your
reward in heaven, for in the same way they persecuted
the prophets who were before you. (verses 5–12)

Jesus speaks blessings over people who are gentle, who dili-
gently seek righteousness, who show mercy, whose hearts are in
the right place, and who make peace. When you are full of
mercy, peace is your first response when you have been wronged.
Those who are not full of mercy would be more interested in
getting back at people who have wronged them. Jesus is looking
for people who would be willing to cover someone who has
messed up. That's what the father in the story of the prodigal son
did for his son; he covered him.

You can't just achieve these characteristics; these are the by-
products of begging and mourning. We say, "Let's be peacemak-
ers." That's a good idea, but you can't set out to just be a
peacemaker. You have to beg the Spirit. When you mourn who
you once were, you become meek, you become humble. When
you thirst for righteousness, you are turned off by injustice. This
is all the inner working of the Holy Spirit.

When you become full of mercy, you don't find yourself angry
at people who do you wrong; you find yourself brokenhearted

for them. Even in your anger, you can respond like God. You can respond in love.

As we continue to read this sermon, Jesus is inviting us to be the salt and the light of the earth. There's a warning attached to that: if salt loses its saltiness, it cannot become salt again. Jesus was speaking to us here. We are the salt of the earth, and the only way for us to remain the salt of the earth is to stay humble. Then we will remain full of light and flavor (see Matthew 5:13–16).

When you are appealing, the people around you are going to want to get on board; they are going to want to get in this race. Remember that grace is not a compact car; grace is a train, an "ark" if you will, with room for everyone to get on board.

When Jesus comes down from this mountain after teaching the Beatitudes, He is instantly approached by a leper. Here we have Jesus showing us how to live out what He has just said. Most people would see a leper who has been marginalized by society and point fingers, making the leper run away because he doesn't belong there. But Jesus, the One full of mercy, doesn't respond like you or I would. Jesus responds in mercy, displaying that even people in the worst condition can be loved (see Matthew 8:1–3).

When Moses came down from the mountain holding the Law and saw the Israelites worshiping another god, he made them melt the gold statue they had made, grind it to powder, then spread it on water and drink it (see Exodus 32:15–20). The punishment fit the crime, but this is a clear demonstration of the difference between God and man. When people have been caught doing something wrong, man says, "You commit the crime; you have to serve the time." Man says, in this case, "You literally have to eat it; you have to swallow your mistakes." But Jesus comes and consumes our mistakes. Both Moses and Jesus climbed a mountain to spend time with God, but when they came down, only One carried the heart of God.

Let's go back to the idea that you should let your light shine. In the story of the prodigal son, the father is the host, and by now everyone is looking around saying he's a good, good father. Look at him: he gave his son the best robe, his old room, a seat at the table. He's treating him kindly. At this point everyone standing around has seen the father in action, and now it all points back to the father. We need to shine our light not so people can see us but so they can see how great God is. Humility is not only good for us to practice, but it's great for God because it positions us to operate in grace. Humility is so unlike our human nature that it is almost proof there must be a God.

Allow me to further add that God looks at you with both love and kindness. It doesn't even matter what your face or heart actually looks like. He simply wants your heart and face focused on Him alone, because He knows that your looking in any other direction would lead you away from Him.

> If My people who are called by My name put away their
> pride and pray, and *look for My face,* and turn from
> their sinful ways, then I will hear from heaven. I will
> forgive their sin, and will heal their land. (2 Chronicles
> 7:14, NLV)

When your soul is searching for more, the last place you should look is away from Jesus! That's where the prodigal son went wrong. That's why he left his house. That's why he walked away from the safety of his father's covering. He foolishly thought there was more for him to experience than what his father could offer.

The reality is, this is not an Old Testament or a New Testament problem. This is the trap that has been set for us over and over again. Satan has been baiting humanity with this very issue since the first family was planted in the garden. The problem for us is that we all do it. When we're working under our own power, when we aren't set on God's face, we focus on the wrong thing. Every. Single. Time.

Too often we wonder what we're missing out on, and our eyes start to wander. We assume there has to be something better *outside* the house, so we entertain the question, "What am I missing?" No one is exempt from this assault. Not you and definitely not me.

Sometime ago my wife and I decided we were going to put our house on the market. We were going to sell our house and search for something better. It was during my quiet time, as I sought His face, that God told me not to sell my house. There was no need to look for anything else; the one we already had was exactly what our family needed. Had I not sought His face, I might have gotten caught in that trap. We have to be intentional about seeking His face so our eyes don't lead us away from what God has for us.

Chapter 9

THE PARTY

The Guest of Honor Might Surprise You

Murder was the only way that
everybody stayed in line. You got
out of line, you got whacked.
Everybody knew the rules.

—Henry Hill (Ray Liotta),
Goodfellas

It would be natural if the prodigal son had expected to be treated harshly, maybe even punished, given the severity of the pain and shame he had caused. He should have been rejected. He could have been relegated to working the dirtiest jobs on his father's property. It's hard to let go of the shame that sin causes, but in the midst of the son's trying to overcome that stinging shame, remember the father's response to the long-lost son as he saw him in the distance. When that day came and he finally saw his son, the one he has missed, the one he has been waiting for, the father does the unimaginable. Without delay and with compassion in his heart, the father runs to meet him. He could not wait for his son to be in the house. He could not wait to wrap his loving arms around him. He could not wait to welcome his son home.

It is almost as if the father was prepared for his son's return. He did not seem to hesitate; he did not wonder what he should do. He didn't force his son to walk through the back door to hide his shame from his neighbors. He didn't berate him for leaving in the first place.

As a dad myself, I can tell you there are times when I have to tell my children what to do and give them no option. I am tempted to put my foot down and demand obedience. There are also times when I know they need to learn for themselves, which ultimately betters them. The father could not force his son to stay in the house, but he wasn't going to keep him out of the house to teach him a lesson. He knew his son had already learned the lesson. He was back, and that was his only concern.

As the father is running toward his dirty son, we see the grace of God racing toward the one who's been weighed down far too long. The father was himself doing the unspeakable; in those days it was not customary for a man to run. Running would require him to pull his own robe up and expose his legs. His response was surprising. I imagine the servants standing around were wondering what the father was thinking. The father bore shame; he allowed himself to be exposed to reconcile his son to himself.

As he reaches him, the son starts to apologize, and it's as if the father doesn't even hear him. He doesn't even seem to be interested in the apology or the explanation the son has prepared. He actually didn't need one. He knows his son's heart has already repented. He quickly calls his servants to bring his son the best robe, a pair of sandals, and a ring. In this moment he is reinstating him as a son of the house. He is covering his shame. He is preparing him to walk correctly.

This is the perfect picture of what our Father's love looks like and how He responds to us. His love doesn't wait for us; it anticipates our return; it reaches out for us. Grace isn't waiting at the door, and it isn't waiting for your acts of contrition or atonement. Grace runs to meet you where you are and covers you completely. Grace allows the sinner to come back home, and it allows you to set your feet in the right direction.

The father wastes no time at all; he sets the party in motion. He doesn't even call the rest of the family to tell them the good news; he immediately calls on his staff to prepare the best celebration. We get to see the face and the heart of God here. God gives us His best even when we are at our worst!

Take the story of Zacchaeus, for example. It's one of my favorite stories in the book of Luke. Jesus is coming into town, and there's quite a ruckus. The crowds have already started to form; people are pushing their way around. They want to see; they want to hear what Jesus has to say. Zacchaeus is curious, but he is too short to see through the crowd. Why was this such a big deal? Luke tells us Zacchaeus is a tax collector, a licensed thief, empowered by the government to betray his own people, steal from them, and report back to the Roman government. Zacchaeus may be small in stature, but he is a small man for other reasons too: he is a known thief and traitor, certified and authorized by the government. He can't see through the crowds. He is curious; he wants to see Jesus. He has no idea Jesus already has His eye on him.

Zacchaeus spots a tree. He winds his way through the crowds to get to that tree. Actually, he probably shoves his way through the crowd, because no one is moving out of the way for this guy. He gets to the tree, climbs up, and starts scanning the crowd for Jesus when Jesus approaches him and calls him out of the tree. Jesus calls his name, "Zacchaeus!" Jesus spots the other thief in the crowd, and He calls him by name.

This is a big deal. Imagine being a short kid walking into junior high school for the first time. New school. New faces. No one knows you. Feeling isolated and alone, you put on a brave face as you walk through those doors. Through the crowd of towering teenagers, you hear someone call your name. Panic and relief rush through your heart and mind as you try to figure out who knows you and why the person is calling you. Is it a friend from elementary school, or could it be the kid you picked on in the fourth grade? So you hold your breath and wait to see how it plays out.

Zacchaeus has no idea his life is about to be turned upside down. Jesus calls Zacchaeus and then invites Himself over for dinner. Yes, Jesus is the friend who invites Himself over for dinner. Imagine the dinner party that Zacchaeus puts together. Who are his friends? They say "birds of a feather flock together."

His buddies are probably the rest of the outcasts of his town: the town thieves, liars, and prostitutes.

That must have been one colorful conversation around the table. Not knowing who Jesus was, assuming He was one of them, they must have told some interesting jokes and stories. Zacchaeus must have been nervous. His mind must have been racing: *What is He doing here? What could He want from me?*

Across the table Jesus is sitting back listening to the debate Zacchaeus is having in his mind. Jesus is probably smiling as He thinks, *You're not even that good of a thief, Zacchaeus. What I am about to steal from you will knock your sandals off. You climbed a tree to see Me, and I'm about to climb a tree to free you.*

This dinner party changes the game for Zacchaeus and the people in their town. By the end of their time together, Zacchaeus is a changed man. I bet he never imagined when he woke up that day that his life would be changed. I bet he never expected Jesus would come looking for him in his current state. Now he is planning to make everything right with the people in his community.

Grace pursued Zacchaeus when he was stealing from his own people; it went home with him for dinner. Grace pursues the sinner with compassion, with the goal of bringing hope, new life, restoration, and transformation. Grace pursues us when we are on the run. Grace doesn't come to devour us; grace shows up to get us back on the right path, toward our purpose and predestined calling. Grace shows up for the prodigal son, and grace will show up for you.

What Zacchaeus and the prodigal son didn't know is that the Father is never too busy for the one who's far off or the one who's close. There's no distance Jesus isn't willing to travel for any of His own: the one running from Him, the one who is curious, and the one who has no idea who He is. What continually gets me is that He doesn't wait for us to be back in the house, all cleaned up with a full explanation or an apology ready. While Justice demands punishment, Grace says, "I already paid for this, so let's just enjoy the party!"

Jesus knew that even at our best we wouldn't come to Him, so instead He comes to us. He used Hosea to go after Gomer, He used an angel to go after Jacob, and in the parable of the prodigal son, He is Himself running toward the wayward son. He is relentless in His pursuit of every single one of us.

In the story of the prodigal son, while the father is busy celebrating, there is someone else who has been affected by all of this. Big brother is in the house, and his response tells us he is bothered that little brother is allowed back home. Why did it bother him so much that he refused to go into the party even after his father came out to personally invite him to the celebration?

Big brother, the son who stayed home and fulfilled his responsibilities, the one who made better choices and did the right thing, is around, but he isn't too happy. As he approaches the house and realizes there is a party going on, we see just how bothered he is by his father's forgiving spirit. He is furious that his disrespectful little brother, who spent his father's money on prostitutes, is allowed back home, so why would his father throw him a party?

As we finish reading the story, it's clear he is upset because he has been good, he has done what was required, he stayed the course. Now his brother, who has done everything wrong, is getting a welcome-home party. He becomes angry with his father for killing the fatted calf, the animal that was on reserve for a special occasion. Little brother messed up; he didn't deserve this elaborate response from their father.

Little brother wasn't good enough. He didn't earn his father's love or forgiveness, but neither could big brother, and neither can you or I. We were NEVER good enough. The surprising truth is, there are no degrees of behavior in God's justice system. There is no sin that could cause us to be permanently cut off from our heavenly Father. Some of us struggle to believe that and receive that. Ultimately, those of us who can't believe it or receive it have an issue with grace.

We should be careful of the Christians who question the salvation of a Christian who might have spent some time in the pigpen. Regardless of where people come from or the stench they carry, we have to be ready to celebrate their salvation and their return home.

> We have all become like one who is unclean,
>   and all our righteous deeds are like a polluted
>   garment.
> We all fade like a leaf,
>   and our iniquities, like the wind, take us
>   away. (Isaiah 64:6, ESV)

Isaiah reminds us that on our best day we are all like the prodigal son, in need of the Father's mercy and forgiveness. And on our worst day, when we forget what it is like to carry the consequences of sin and the guilt and shame it brings, we can also be like the older brother who could not bring himself inside to celebrate the return of his younger brother.

Christians, let's never forget where we were when we first encountered Jesus and what we were saved from. When we forget that we were once sinners in need of forgiveness, in need of freedom from the shackles of past mistakes, we become the worst kind of Christians—the kind of Christians who make it impossible for people who carry guilt and shame to come back home. When we forget how hard it was to live with guilt and shame, when we forget where we once were, we are easily repulsed by people who have not yet received grace.

I heard a story about a man who was homeless and had probably had a few beers before he went to an outreach event hosted by a local church. The goal of the event was to reach people in the community they hadn't reached before. After enjoying a picnic in the park, listening to Christian musicians and artists sing and dance all afternoon, he responded when he heard the gospel preached. He remained in his seat because he wasn't steady on his feet. A "Christian" came over to pray for him, inhaled once, and immediately got up and walked away. He must have forgotten that he had once stepped in some stuff. He must have forgotten that he once smelled of the stench of sin. He must have forgotten how he felt the first time he heard that Jesus loved him. Surely he forgot how heavy his sin once was, how it had weighed on him, and what it felt like when he was then able to stand up straight for the first time.

When we become the kind of person who denies someone else the opportunity to become clean, we become the religious Pharisees that Jesus referred to as "whitewashed tombs." We may be clean on the outside, but on the inside we are like empty tombs with nothing to offer except the "bones of the dead and everything unclean" (Matthew 23:27). I would always question the salvation of the Christian who has an issue with people being saved or who won't celebrate salvation.

Let's not forget who was in the audience while Jesus was telling this story. In addition to the tax collectors and the prostitutes, the Pharisees, who were blinded by their "rightness," were also on site. They were often part of Jesus's audience.

Jesus, the rabbi (teacher), the master communicator and orator, was not only speaking to the "notorious sinners" (Luke 15:1, NLT) but was also speaking to the older brothers in the audience, the religious ones who made right choices. Jesus not only intended for them to hear this story, but He made them part of the story too.

The father in the story of the prodigal son knew that if he gave his son enough time and space, he would eventually find his way back home. If we could look around this house, we might have seen that the father had a robe hanging in the front closet on the hook closest to the door, that the calf had already been fatted. The father was not only hoping for his son's return; he was planning on it, and he was prepared to cover him and celebrate when he arrived.

These brothers represent two kinds of Christians. There's the brother who stays in the house and the brother who wanders off looking for more.

We become like the older brother, forgetting we were once like the younger brother and struggled to figure out where we belonged, when we are impatient with the brother who wanders off and then are repulsed by his stench when he comes back.

We are most like the younger brother, the one whose eyes wandered outside of the home and looked for more even though he already had everything he needed, the one who walked away but is now in need of a loving father.

By the end of the party, we realize that while the older brother was around fulfilling his obligations, he was also far off from where he should have been. Sure, he was home taking care of family business and being responsible, but his heart was far off. He was unforgiving. He could not celebrate that his brother, who was once lost, had now been found. He also was in need of the father. He, like the Pharisees, didn't see or understand that Jesus was calling him back to Himself too. His heart was not forgiving.

Do you see yourself in this parable? This might be the perfect time for you to reflect on why you understood the prodigal son felt that he couldn't go home. Maybe you understand the rage the older brother felt. Or maybe you just need to accept the fact that your Father already has your robe hanging in the front closet, the table is set, and all you have to do is let Him cover you.

If we can be real here, let's talk about the father for a minute and how he is the real hero in this story. While he was the one who threw the party for his son, he's really the one everyone is celebrating, because he allowed the son to come back home. Yes, they are celebrating the son's homecoming, but that could not have happened if the father wasn't prepared to forgive the son.

There is nothing that makes God happier than to see His people celebrating His character. In the beginning of this book, we talked about how God wants our worship, our praise, and how Satan wants to steal that from Him. It's God's grace that allows us to worship despite our failures. It's one thing to fight through forgiveness; it's another to forgive. Have you ever felt you had to forgive someone when you really didn't want to because you were justified in being upset? We justify our anger; God justifies forgiveness, and God's ultimate goal is to get the glory.

THE GLORY OF GOD

When Lazarus, Jesus's friend, gets sick, Mary and Martha send word to Jesus (see John 11:1–3). They believe that if Jesus comes to them, He will heal Lazarus. Jesus stays where He is and doesn't go to their home until Lazarus has been dead for four days. He says, "This sickness will not end in death. No, it is for God's glory so that God's Son may be glorified through it" (verse 4). Martha is so grief stricken by what she sees that she cannot believe the message.

Life will do that to us too. Sometimes we can be so affected by the everyday (for example, the doctor's report, the bank balance, the pink slip, the status change, the news, the uncertainty, and so on) that we doubt the Word, God's Word.

Martha met Jesus as He arrived in Bethany; then she went

home to Mary and told her Jesus was asking for her. When Mary ran out to meet Him, she had her own message to deliver. She fell at His feet and wept. She told Him that He was too late; if He had only been there sooner her brother would be alive (see verses 20–32). Mary was so fixated on the situation that it was all she could see; the story her human eyes told her was that Jesus was too late.

John 11:33–35 tells us that when Jesus saw her and the Jews who were with her weeping, He also wept. It makes sense to hear of people weeping when a loved one dies. It's natural and expected. But this wasn't about grieving the loss of a brother or the loss of a friend. Could it be that Jesus was grief stricken by the fact that Mary was in the presence of God Himself yet missed seeing the glory of God? Anytime we look at Jesus we should see the glory of God.

Technically, at this point, Mary too was an unbeliever. Jesus had told Martha that Lazarus would rise again, but she thought He was telling her about the distant future. Could this be why when Jesus finally arrived at the tomb, He wept (see verse 35)? Jesus wanted these sisters to know that Lazarus would live again. He wanted them to believe His word. Jesus didn't cry because He was grieving over Lazarus. He was crying because they didn't recognize fully who He was and didn't trust that His word wouldn't return void (see Isaiah 55:11, NKJV). They knew Him as Jesus but failed to see Him as God. The god of this age blinded the minds of the unbelievers.

When we fail to see the glory of God, our Father is grieved. However, when our Father sees His children celebrating His goodness, He is pleased. When our Father prepares a celebration for an undeserving son, it points to God's glory. I say this with reverence: God is crazy enough to forgive all men and all women so there will be no wall or blockage from Him getting His glory. He'd rather forgive you than punish you because there's no glory in punishment. There is, however, glory in forgiveness, which is why He gives grace.

The next thing Jesus did was call Lazarus from his grave (see John 11: 43). He fulfilled His word. Jesus is showing us that even when we fail to see Him, He is still God and He still does what He said He would do.

This isn't the first time we see Jesus welcome everyone to the party. What about the Last Supper? We all know who was at the table with Him.

When Jesus starts planning the Passover meal, He invites His disciples, all of them. He doesn't single out just the good guys or the disciples who have been the most faithful. He is sitting around that table with His whole crew. That's when He drops the bombshell on them. As He is reclining at the table, He announces that one of them is going to betray Him. His demeanor is worth noting. He isn't flipping tables this time.

He isn't angry. He isn't panic stricken, looking for the mole. He's not throwing anyone out. He simply states a fact: someone in His inner circle is going to betray Him.

Imagine finding yourself in that situation, knowing someone you have trusted to work so closely with you was about to turn you in and that the betrayal would set your death in motion. Would you allow that person to have Passover dinner with you? Would this disciple be allowed at the table with you? Would you be able to relax at the table knowing the end was near?

> You prepare a table before me
>> in the presence of my enemies.
> You anoint my head with oil;
>> my cup overflows.
> Surely your goodness and love will follow me
>> all the days of my life,
> and I will dwell in the house of the LORD
>> forever. (Psalm 23:5–6)

As far as Jesus is concerned, there's a place for everybody at the table, and they are all welcome at the party. His haters are welcome, His persecutors are welcome, the one who steals from Him is welcome, and the adulteress is welcome too. Like King David, Jesus was okay with sitting at the table with His enemies.

This is what separates Jesus from most thieves. In most of the movies I've seen about thieves, they are very careful about the company they keep. They want to make sure they are surrounding themselves with people who can be trusted to keep secrets and not crack under pressure. Having the wrong person on his team was probably the only reason Notarbartolo was caught. Speedy panicked and got sloppy. He tossed garbage in the wrong place with just enough information in it to point the authorities in the right direction. Some loose diamonds and a half-eaten sandwich with Notarbartolo's DNA led police right to him.

King David helps us understand how Jesus was able to invite Judas to dinner. Jesus wasn't afraid to sit at the table with tax collectors, sinners, and ultimately the person who would sell Him out for a few pieces of silver. He didn't seem to be concerned about the consequences of having at the table the man who would betray Him and set His death in motion.

Before we question why Jesus was a turn-the-cheek kind of man, let's remember that Jesus was also purpose driven. As a little boy, when He was accidentally left behind in Jerusalem one Passover, He said to Mary and Joseph, "Did you not know that I must be about My Father's business?" (Luke 2:49, NKJV). When He talked about the reason He came, to give life abundantly, He followed that up by explaining that a good shepherd lays down his life for his sheep (see John 10:10–11). Everything He had done until this point has shown us He was purpose driven. He knew His time on earth was limited, so He made the most of it. And He wasn't afraid of Judas. In fact, to some extent Jesus needed Judas in order to fulfill His purpose.

We can't be the kind of people who panic when we find there are haters are among us. Sometimes we need the haters and the people who test us to propel us toward our purpose. Have you ever looked up at the sky during the day and seen stars? It's not possible. During the day the sky reflects the light of the sun reflecting off the water. Stars can only be seen on a clear night when the sky is dark, and the darker the night, the brighter the stars.

This is why Jesus is telling the story of the prodigal son to the peasants, liars, cheaters, common folk, *and* the Pharisees. The father in the story of the prodigal son shines even brighter against the backdrop of his judgmental son. We need the bad guys in the story of our lives to bring our purpose to light, to let our light shine bright for Jesus.

Jesus was not off to the side in a private place and out of sight. He was out in the open. The Pharisees, who likely gathered to hear Jesus's teachings regularly, were there. They wanted to listen, but they seemed to be distracted. They couldn't understand why Jesus, a rabbi, would allow such people to sit with Him. How could He be so welcoming to the wicked, and out in the open, no less? This was no accident. I'm pretty sure He intended for them to hear this story. This was likely a tactical move.

Sitting with the notorious wasn't new to Him; He seemed to attract all kinds of people. Jesus never seemed to shy away from anyone—not the good, the bad, or the ugly. This day was no different.

Both sons were present in the story, both sons were present when Jesus told the story, and as it turns out, both sons represent all of humanity, the believer and the nonbeliever.

Those listening did not sneak into a closed session. They might have thought they did, but Jesus purposely allowed them to be there because this message of hope was just as much for the one who considers himself a good son as it is for the adulterer, the betrayer who runs away. This is a living illustration and example that where sin abounds, grace abounds all the more (see Romans 5:20). This is also an illustration of the Mastermind who dwelt among the people before He pulled off His own heist.

NOT THE SAME KIND OF TURN UP— AN OPEN INVITATION

The prodigal son had gone to some parties while he was away, probably some of the best parties anyone had seen, but I am also guessing all the parties were similar: red plastic cups, a cool DJ, drugs, dirty dancing orchestrated by vulgar music, and some hooking up.

The party he was invited to at the end of the story was a different party. It was the real party. The other parties wished they could be like this one. Although they all included things that seemed to be entertaining or fun, they left him tired, spent, and ashamed. There's no comparing the homecoming party to the parties thrown by money-hungry promoters or people with the same emptiness as the prodigal; although they seemed to offer fun times, those parties were empty because they couldn't offer anything more than what they already possessed: emptiness.

This party was thrown by a man who had more than the son did: food, location, and servants that all *belonged* to him, which meant they couldn't be shut down for public disturbance because some superior owner came home or even because they would run out of food or resources. This party offered all those things and symbolized acceptance and happiness. There was no entrance fee, because now that the son was willing to walk into the party, he had the full right to enjoy it.

The only problem with this party was that it created a problem for other party promoters: they couldn't compete. See, it's one thing to crash a party, but it's a whole different game when you steal guests who had RSVP'd to another party.

This party is filled with life: good music, good punch, and good food—metaphors for life and living. Life is to be enjoyable, and we are *all* able to enjoy it. The only way people don't get into the party is if they choose not to come in. The older brother, aka the "Good One," refused to go, and the younger brother, aka the "Sinful One," was not only at the party but was probably dancing in the middle.

THE REAL GUEST OF HONOR

The party was more for the dad than it was for the son. Jesus and the dad are the same person. The dad is the picture of the gospel. What was the dad's motive for allowing the son to come back home? The dad was all the son had; the son had nowhere else to turn.

The father experienced the shame just as Jesus experienced shame. The father ran. He wasn't supposed to.

If the dad was the only person who could help the son, that means his brother wasn't going to help him. God knew He was the only One who could help us because man couldn't help man. He was the only One who could get the job done.

Leaders, brothers, sisters, friends, may we always be the kind of Christians who will celebrate the return of the lost, because God gave us His best when we were at our worst. If God gave us His best at our worst, then *we* have to give our best to those who find themselves at their worst, in the midst of their worst behavior.

I hope we never forget where God brought us from—our

stench, our hunger, and our heartache—or the relief we felt when He took the weight of our shame. Christians who forget about their journey to Jesus or the stuff they were saved from become the worst kind of Christian. When we make the mistake of forgetting what we were and where we came from, we are repulsed by the stench of others.

We have all needed to take that walk to Jesus with all our stuff and our stink. Some of us have made that journey back home once, and some of us have had to make that trip back to Jesus on more than one occasion. Whether we've made that journey once or twenty times, the end is always the same. Every time we left and finally had to return, we were met with the same love by the same Father, who each time came running toward us and covered us. The grace of God is something we may never understand, but we don't have to. Our only responsibility is to fully accept it. The Mastermind's mind is made up about you; He was determined to love you from before He formed you. That is why He gives us so many opportunities to come back.

I'm glad the father got to his younger son before his big brother could give him a piece of his mind. Can you imagine the ugly exchange and the accusations?

When little brother left, big brother had to stay home and watch the sadness and disappointment in his father's eyes. He probably watched him sitting by the window, looking for his son to appear in the distance. He likely heard the weeping and prayers that came from his father's room at night. It wouldn't surprise me if the older brother had plenty to say about how his younger brother broke his father's heart.

Unfortunately, there are big brothers among us, in our churches, in our communities, even in our families, who are all too ready to tell the backsliders how much they stink and what ingrates they are for having left in the first place. There is nothing worse than when people in their worst behavior have to deal with religious, pharisaical Christians in their behavior. Grace exchanges our worst behavior for His endless grace.

This is what makes God the ultimate Mastermind. He had a well-thought-out plan from the very beginning. A plan that included covering the younger brother's stench, the sinner who is far off, welcoming him home at his worst. A plan that includes the older brother, the religious one who seems to be doing the right thing on the outside but is clearly bothered by the mistakes of the one who isn't as wise on the inside. A plan that puts Jesus, the most righteous and holy of thieves, on a wooden cross, stealing our shame and sorrow so the Father can welcome us home.

IT'S NOT A COMPETITION

Jesus's three years of ministry were not necessarily about healing people and rescuing them; He could have done that from heaven. His reason for healing and rescuing was to show everyone that *anyone* can be healed or rescued—we all could be saved. As you look at all the people Jesus encountered, you see that no one was excluded. For three years He was on His own stakeout. He was watching us, walking with us, experiencing what we experience in our everyday lives. His intent was to steal the shame and sting not only of sin but of any ideas that would combat opportunities for grace, including the idea that we have to earn healing or restoration.

The Father's goal was to save the one who realizes he needs a Savior and to give grace to the one who thinks she's been making all the right decisions. He wants to give us more grace when we fail, and He wants us to celebrate the one who returns home.

Jesus was showing us that He is not limited to the confines of a temple; He took His ministry to the streets and into the homes of some misfits. He showed us that we can approach a sinful woman at a well, not to scorn her, but to lovingly show her all the things she has done and to offer life-giving water, an alternative to the lifestyle she has been living. We can eat and hang with tax collectors (government officials, also known as the certified thieves of the time) and prostitutes. He showed us that we can change the environment; the environment does not have to change us.

When you have a real revelation of grace, your mind is set on the truth. You're in love with the truth and grace, and anything that opposes truth and grace bothers you to the point of action.

We need to see more Christians leaving the safety of the four walls of churches and going out to where the people are: at parties, in drug-infested neighborhoods, in the local park.

Grace will overpower sin, because where sin is, grace is there too. Grace fulfills what man is actually looking for sin to fulfill. So go where the sin is, not to sin but to share another option. Go with the confidence that what you know and who you know will give the people the fulfillment they've been looking for.

GRACE ALWAYS WAS

Grace is the undeserved, unmerited favor of God. Grace gives you and me immediate access to a Holy God in our current state. But grace does not first appear on the scene in Bethlehem or at Calvary. Grace was in the garden in Genesis. Grace gave Noah the opportunity to try to save some of humanity. Grace made it possible for Moses to go back up the mountain and get a new set of tablets when he destroyed the first tablets in his rage. Grace allowed King Solomon to take over the throne after King David's family suffered the consequences of David's sin.

If God knew Adam and Eve would choose the wrong thing, why would He allow them in the garden in the first place? If He knew you and I would make as many bad choices as we have, why would He give us life? Why would He call us? Why would He give us purpose, knowing full well that at some point we would all trip and fail? The answer is as simple and as complicated as the question. God allowed them in the garden because we all needed free will, and when Adam and Eve eventually failed, God responded by confronting them with grace as He covered both Adam and Eve (see Genesis 3:21).

The father in the story of the prodigal son knew that if he gave his son enough time and space, he would eventually find his way back home. When the son finally returned, the father didn't berate him for leaving; he didn't force him to come in through the back door. The father did the unspeakable: he ran to meet his son, and he covered him. That is the perfect picture of what our heavenly Father's love looks like. His love reaches for you, wherever you are, and covers you. Grace isn't waiting at the door; grace runs to meet you where you are and covers you completely.

> But God demonstrates his own love for us in this: While
> we were still sinners, Christ died for us. (Romans 5:8)

Scripture shows us that we are all bound to sin. In our fallen humanity, it is not possible to be perfect. God's Law was given to us so that all people could see how sinful we are. But as people sinned more and more, God's wonderful grace became more abundant. Grace flows from a well that cannot run dry. It hasn't expired. Grace was not limited to Old Testament stories or New

Testament parables. God's grace is a present-day gift available to all of us, the sinner and the saint, the child who leaves and the child who stays, the one who runs to sin and the one who makes every effort to do the right thing.

LOOKING DOWN

When an older brother looks down on you and suggests you're not good enough, you can easily get pulled into believing you really aren't good enough, unless you're renewing your mind.

A few years ago I had the privilege of speaking at the closing session of a five-day leaders' conference overseas. Thousands of people were in attendance. I felt honored to have been invited to speak, but I have to admit I had some reservations. I didn't speak their language, and I was unsure of how my message would translate. I was also the youngest speaker in the lineup.

My session ended, and with that, the conference came to a close. I received encouraging words from many of the pastors who gathered in the greenroom following the session. I was feeling pretty good about the events of the week. My message was very well received. We experienced a real God moment. Actually, the session was even better than I could have hoped. That is, until my eyes locked with one of the visiting pastors. He walked into the greenroom, headed directly toward me, but then suddenly sat down. He proceeded to call me over to him. My body tensed as I walked, and I wondered, *Did I offend him?* Was something not translated properly? Did I misquote Scripture? Where could I have gone wrong? I knew this was not going to be good.

As I approached, he began to tell me that I had delivered, in his opinion, a "great message." He told me he thought I had a gift to communicate, but he also wanted to inform me that I had used a word incorrectly. He continued to explain that he was offended I would suggest that Jesus pulled a heist. This preacher (who was also a lawyer) clarified, explaining that *heist* has a negative connotation. I later looked it up to try to understand why he felt so strongly about it that he would make his way to me just to tell me. According to the Cambridge Dictionary, a *heist* is "a crime in which valuable things are taken illegally and often violently from a place or person."

He may have had the best of intentions. Although his tone was a bit condescending, he meant well. His decision to challenge me in front of all the other visiting pastors and leaders in the greenroom led me to a brief moment of insecurity. I guess we've all experienced in one way or another an older brother challenging us because he wants us to know about the mistake he believes we have made. I heard my father's voice in my head, reminding me to treat every older man with respect, and I sensed the Holy Spirit telling me to ignore his statements, so I graciously thanked him for his feedback and walked away.

I responded as my father would have wanted me to, but if I didn't lay down that insecurity right away, if I didn't guard my heart and mind against what seemed to be a rebuke by the older brother, I might have derailed my purpose.

In a room full of people, I imagine it would be pretty easy to find people who've had to make the same decision, but we might also find people who hadn't. We choose to believe what God has said about us instead of what someone in the house—a sibling, a leader, a deacon, a friend—might say about us. It's no secret what God says about us. Let's be careful to store those truths in our hearts so we don't make the wrong decision or the kind of decisions that will rob us of our purpose and our destiny when an older brother confronts us.

TURF WARS

Imagine walking through gang turf, a specific street or a section of the park taken over by a group of guys wearing the same colors or bandannas. I'm not talking about your local cheerleaders; I'm talking about tough guys, scary-looking guys, the kind of guys who make it clear you do not belong anywhere near them. So you cross the street because you don't want to say or do anything that will offend one of them. Now imagine a bigger gang wearing a different color showing up at that block or in that section of the park, looking to take over that turf and claim it for their own. There's a scuffle, and gang number one is overpowered. They are stripped of their colors and their clothes, stripped of their power and pride, and sent out of the park naked. To say it would be embarrassing would be an understatement.

Those guys would no longer be a threat, at least not while they're running around naked and bruised. Their nakedness and bruises would prove they weren't as big and bad as they had appeared or threatened to be.

This is what God did to Satan when he started stirring up trouble in heaven and God threw him out. It is what Jesus did to death when He rose from the grave. It is what grace does to sin and the shame of sin every time sin shows up. Sin is powerless in our lives once it's been stripped naked. It is the reason I had to write this book, to make sure you understand that grace wins. Grace beats the pants off of sin and sends shame running every single time. We just have to be willing to receive it.

Grace isn't just for a good son, and it isn't just for a bad son. When Jesus was lifted on that cross, He leveled the playing field. He made grace available to anyone who would receive it. That's why a father can throw an over-the-top party for a son who fails miserably and comes back home. Grace is also the reason a father can go outside and invite the stubborn good son into the party too.

Chapter 10

THE GOODS

What You Get to Keep

You're gonna get us all pinched.

—James Conway (Robert DeNiro),
Goodfellas

In the movie *Goodfellas,* a team of professional thieves makes its living stealing and selling loot. This is a classic mobster movie about these thieves working their way up to their big heist. They steal $4 million from an airport. This was no easy task, but they planned carefully and prepared for every level of security. They had a guy working on the inside, they knew who would go in and get the money, and they planned the getaway. They didn't get caught, but they couldn't enjoy what they did. They had to stay under the radar; otherwise they'd give themselves away. This was a rule they couldn't compromise on. Extravagant spending could blow their cover. In one scene one of the mobsters' wives buys a pink fur. She loves this fur and wants to show it off, so she wears it out in public. One of the mob bosses loses his cool when he sees it. The rules of the heist were simple: pull off the job and lie low to remain undetected.

The lives of professional thieves must be frustrating. They can pull off the most complex heist, but they can't brag about it, they can't talk about it, and no one can ever know, or they risk getting caught. They live lives of secrecy. They have to be some of the smartest criminals if they don't want to get caught, but they can't celebrate openly. No one can know. They don't get to brag, and they don't get to enjoy it.

Successful thieves will take their time with surveillance; before they take on a job, they have to be smart and anticipate every possible scenario. Their timing has to be well calculated, and the getaway is just as important as the heist itself. It has to be well timed, and the thieves have to minimize the potential for surprises in the escape route.

Remember, however, that Jesus had Judas and David had Saul. When you begin to operate in your calling, the haters, the persecutors, the naysayers are all going to show up. Don't let them scare you or intimidate you. The Judases and Sauls of this world should not scare you. They should encourage you! Had David not spent so much time on the run and hiding in caves, he would have been a different person. His prayer and worship life were forever impacted by his time on the run. The author of Psalm 23 knew about sitting with his enemies, and he will be forever known as a man after God's own heart (see 1 Samuel 13:14; Acts 13:22). Jesus needed Judas to betray Him so He could fulfill His purpose. In Luke 6, Jesus tells us we are blessed when people hate us, exclude us, and reject us because of Him (see verse 22). Hard steps always cause us to question our calling, but really it's those steps that may affirm our calling. What looks like failure may really be fulfillment.

We can't think about David without thinking about his nemesis, Saul. Saul was an epic villain, a proud man. He hated that David was going to take his place. He tried to kill David on more than one occasion and even pretended he was just kidding around. He wasn't stable. He was jealous, and Saul made David's life so miserable that David went running for his life.

While Saul was no great example, David, the man after God's own heart, was also a flawed man. Measured against our human standards, David's failures may outweigh his successes. David sat around entertaining his wandering eye when he should have been with his men in battle. He lusted after another man's wife. He fathered a child with that man's wife, and then to cover up his sin, he committed murder when he sent the man to the front lines, knowing full well the man would not come home to his family. David failed to protect his daughter's honor when she was assaulted. He struggled with anxiety and fear and spent time on the run.

What's more incredible than the name given to David—a man after God's own heart—is the name given to Jesus. He was known as the "Son of David." When we read David's rap sheet, we have to wonder why Jesus would want to be associated with David. The answer is simple. David humbled himself time and time again before God. He had no problem getting down low and repenting with a sincere heart. In Psalm 103 we see proof that David understood forgiveness as he prayed, "As far as the east is from the west, so far does he remove our transgressions from us" (verse 12, ESV). David understood that while he was flawed and continually failed, God's grace was ultimately greater.

Do you know how many times you have disqualified yourself because you have made too many mistakes? Because your clothes carry the stench of years of sin? Because you have been listening to the voices of those around you who have labeled you as something other than a child of God? Because of who you are or what you have done? These are all lies; they're the tactics Satan will use to keep you from stepping into your destiny, to keep you from believing that God has any use for you.

SIMON PETER'S RESPONSE

You may be wondering how David accepted God's grace so easily. Was he giving himself a pass, or did he have a different level of insight than we have? It is not that difficult to receive what God has for us. In one of my favorite passages, we see Simon Peter struggling to receive what God had for him.

One day as Jesus was standing by the Lake of Gennesaret, the people were crowding around him and listening to the word of God. He saw at the water's edge two boats, left there by the fishermen, who were washing their nets. He got into one of the boats, the one belonging to Simon, and asked him to put out a little from shore. Then he sat down and taught the people from the boat.

When he had finished speaking, he said to Simon, "Put out into deep water, and let down the nets for a catch."

Simon answered, "Master, we've worked hard all night and haven't caught anything. But because you say so, I will let down the nets."

When they had done so, they caught such a large number of fish that their nets began to break. So they signaled their partners in the other boat to come and help them, and they came and filled both boats so full that they began to sink.

When Simon Peter saw this, he fell at Jesus' knees and said, "Go away from me, Lord; I am a sinful man!" For he and all his companions were astonished at the catch of fish they had taken, and so were James and John, the sons of Zebedee, Simon's partners.

Then Jesus said to Simon, "Don't be afraid; from now on you will fish for people." So they pulled their boats up on shore, left everything and followed him. (Luke 5:1–11)

Simon had been working all night, dropping heavy, two-hundred-foot nets overboard in hopes of making a great catch. He waited. He pulled up the nets, found nothing but seaweed, and tossed the nets back in. He repeated these steps over and over again. This was the process.

By the time Jesus is wrapping up His teaching, Simon is tired and probably frustrated. He had been at it for hours: tossing the nets, coming up empty, cleaning the nets, and tossing them out again. This was strenuous, physically and emotionally. Does this scene sound familiar? Have you ever had to repeat the same process over and over again, hoping for a change but finding you are wasting your time while your passion is dwindling and your dreams are fading?

Simon wants to call it quits. He's beat. There would be no big catch today. As he is getting ready to pack it up, Jesus stops him. He asks Simon to take a risk. He tells Simon to drop the nets again in deep water. Simon responds based on what he has seen. Can you see him rolling his eyes and saying, "You've been here all day. You know there are no fish down there, but I don't want to argue with You. I'm too tired. I'll do it again only because You asked."

Simon's response shouldn't be shocking. He didn't say anything you and I haven't said when we've been up against a wall. "God, I know You don't want this marriage to end, but I've done all I can. I'm throwing in the towel." Or you've been struggling with an addiction so long that when you hear God inviting you to receive a fresh start, you think it is a total waste of time to even try. Have you ever told God He is wasting His time with you? Frustration, insecurity, past failures, and exhaustion can cause you to respond like Simon.

God doesn't want our excuses; He is looking for our obedience. He is looking for our yes. He is looking for us to take a risk and trust Him. He is looking to show us what we can do when He is in the boat with us, when He is leading us.

Simon's initial response may not seem very confident, but he doesn't argue, and he ultimately does what Jesus asks him to do. Simon reminds Jesus that he hasn't been successful, as if Jesus needs reminders about our past successes or failures. Simon is feeling insecure and defeated, but he agrees to obey. That's the moment Simon receives grace. That's the sacred moment in this story.

This is the moment Jesus is waiting for. He waits to hear the sound of surrender from Simon, and He waits to hear the sound of surrender from us. The moment when we agree we may have gotten it all wrong in the past, but we are going to obey "because you say so." Living in the grace of God is never about the actual task He is calling us to complete. Living in the grace of God is knowing we don't deserve His grace but receiving it anyway and confidently responding when He calls us.

I may have been unsuccessful, but because You say so, Lord, I am going to try one more time.

I may have failed You more times than I care to remember, but because You say so, Lord, I am not only going to believe I am forgiven, but I am going to walk in the confidence of the freedom Your grace offers.

I may have always had trouble in school, but because You say so, Lord, I am choosing to believe that You have a great plan for my life.

No matter how guilty we are or how much shame we carry, we can be sure we are loved, forgiven, and redeemed. Grace means that God can still use us—because He said so.

I am no exception. I remember the challenges I faced in my own childhood. When I was in the first grade, a teacher called me stupid. I struggled to speak publicly because I had a stutter. I was eventually diagnosed with ADHD. For a long time I believed what my teacher said about me. I didn't want anyone looking at me, listening to me, or making decisions about what I could or could not do, so I decided for myself. I was tired of trying and not being successful.

I was all too familiar with my limitations. I struggled and tried to hide, yet Jim Cymbala, the senior pastor at the Brooklyn Tabernacle, saw something different in me. My appearance, my size, my stutter didn't stop him from believing what God was showing him about me. When I was young, while I was struggling with what my doctors labeled "disabilities," he told my mother to wait to see how God would use me someday.

I didn't want to set myself up for any more failure, so I disqualified myself and made choices to sabotage my future. I messed around with a lot of girls. I was rebellious. I got high. I rejected what God was calling me to do. I wasn't good enough, and I wanted to prove to God that He was wrong about me.

> But what is God's reply to him [Elijah]? I have kept for
> Myself seven thousand men who have not bowed the
> knee to Baal!
>
> So too at the present time there is a remnant (a small
> believing minority), selected (chosen) by grace (by God's
> unmerited favor and graciousness).
>
> But if it is by grace (His unmerited favor and graciousness), it is no longer conditioned on works or anything
> men have done. Otherwise, grace would no longer be
> grace [it would be meaningless]. (Romans 11:4–6, AMPC)

Here's the humbling truth about God's response to us. When we act as though we have to earn grace, He reminds us that grace isn't something we can work for. It is a gift, freely given, to anyone who would be courageous enough to receive it.

Despite my best efforts He never changed His mind about what He was calling me to do. I gave Him my excuses; He said He wanted me anyway. I finally surrendered, and I have to be honest, I could never have imagined the places He has taken me to or the platforms He has given me to speak on. I don't share that to boast about myself but to boast about God. God looked at me and decided something very different than what I had decided about myself. I struggled because I could not believe that God could have anything special for me. He proved me wrong.

Our obedience brings Him honor. Our joy brings Him joy. When we step into our purpose, it gives Him great pleasure, not because we are getting it right, not because we are busy working, but because we have chosen to be obedient.

When Simon relents to Jesus, he finally makes the kind of catch every fisherman hopes for. There are so many fish he needs help to pull the nets into his boat. Then they fill a second boat. At this point both boats are overloaded with fish.

CHANGE YOUR MIND

In the book of Romans, the writer talks about "the renewing of your mind" (12:2). This is one of the greatest instructions given to Christians, and it is one of the greatest things that can happen to us and for us. To renew or to change our minds is not only to think differently but also to bring our thoughts into alignment with God's thoughts.

When Jesus became sin, He became the bad guy, the thief who stole our sin and shame from us. He also stole from Satan. He stole his ability to taunt us with our shame. Jesus stole our guilt and, in exchange, gave us new life, a life with purpose, a life that ultimately recognizes the glory of God and gives God the worship He deserves.

I hope that while you have read this book, you have lost your mind, literally. I hope you have lost all your old thinking and your old mind-sets. Lose the idea that grace is for a select few. Lose the idea that grace has to be earned. Lose the notion that grace is an archaic concept only relevant in biblical times. Grace always is because God always is. When you seek God's face, you will find yourself looking right at the source of grace—and not just for a brief moment but for a lifetime. God cannot operate outside of grace. GRACE IS GOD! The sooner you accept this truth, the quicker you will fall in line with God's master plan. Lose the old mind-set and allow God to give you a new mind-set, because He already stole the shame of your sin, and a life abundant and full of purpose is waiting for you.

I love what Jesus said to Simon when the fisherman pushed the Teacher away: "Don't be afraid; from now on you will fish for people" (Luke 5:10). Jesus gave Simon purpose instantly. One minute Simon was a sinful man, and the next minute he was being used by God. This is an illustration of just how extreme grace is. Grace pursues you even when you have run out of hope. Grace pursues you when you are exhausted and you think you have nothing left to give. When Peter was at his worst, Grace pursued him, and as he responded, he received Jesus's best.

Purpose does not have to be so complicated. Walking in your purpose does not require a degree in theology. Purpose is not a career or a title. You cannot earn your purpose, and you don't have to be perfect to walk in your purpose. Purpose gives direction to your calling. Simon's career was set: he was a fisherman, and Jesus was not giving him a new job. Jesus was inviting him to use the skills he already had and giving him a new mission. To have purpose does not mean we are going to be the next president, CEO, or Mother Teresa. When you have God's purpose and pursue Him passionately, you can become those things, but a global platform is not a requirement for fulfilling your purpose. Simon didn't fill out an application. He did not change his ways on his own. All he had to do was receive what Jesus was offering: purpose.

When we adjust our thinking to start accepting what God says to us, what He says about us, what He says about Himself, then we can celebrate the fact that Jesus stole our sin and shame so we can enjoy the gift of grace. The Bible says, as a man thinks, so he is (see Proverbs 23:7). You can stop thinking you are a failure because you failed. You are not a victim; you are a conqueror in Christ.

May we be a generation that has the courage to allow the heist and ask God to order our steps so we can move toward His purpose for our lives. May we be a generation that responds with a YES!

ACKNOWLEDGMENTS

When I first had the idea to write *The Heist,* I was excited but uncertain about the reception it would receive. I was excited because I felt it was a fresh perspective that would help people understand how powerful the finished work of the Cross really is. I was uncertain because the topics of *grace* and *glory* aren't something a young, newbie author would write about, especially one without a degree in theology. Some of you may be thinking, *"You're not a new author, you wrote Misfit!"* True, but *Misfit* was a book geared toward teenagers and didn't use such provocative illustrations as *The Heist* to make its point. This time around was very different from my previous experience. I'm grateful for several people whom I spoke with to gain much needed perspective along the way: my wife, my parents, my brothers, and friends.

I want to thank my wife, Yahris, and my children, Dylan and Chloe Durso, for releasing me to write this book and for supporting me each step of the way. I can't love you anymore than I do, especially you Yahris Durso. Your love and strength inspire me daily.

To my parents and Senior Pastors—Pastor Michael and Maria Durso—for supporting me, empowering me, and loving me as you do. I couldn't have asked for better parents and pastors. I love you!

To Jordan Durso, thank you for your constant support and encouragement. Your bravery to be different matched with your willingness to "break the rules" always makes me feel less nervous about my crazy ideas, especially when it came to this one.

To Ralph Castillo, I'm so thankful for all our conversations on theology. You have lent me your brilliance more than I've credited. When I first brought this concept to you, you not only encouraged me, but you took the time to dissect it with me. Thank you.

To my brothers, James "Ping Ping" Morales and Abad "Junior" Rivera, I need you both in my life. James, you make me dream bigger, and Junior, you show me how to make my dreams a reality. James, you're always willing to step out with me no matter what that looks like, and Junior, you are too, but you also know where to step, how to step, and when to step. I don't know where my family or I would be without you both.

Rich Wilkerson Jr., thank you for constantly challenging me to strive for excellence. I always walk away from our weekly chats with notes of adjustments and new ideas. When I first brought this concept to you on that flight from Miami to New York City, you challenged me to make this concept more palatable, which caused me to break down this idea further. Thank you!

Thank you, Erwin McManus, for writing the foreword and being a constant inspiration to me. Your willingness to support, encourage, and challenge me has changed my approach on both leading and living. I'm forever grateful for you and your voice in my life.

Thank you, Andrew Stoddard, and the whole WaterBrook Multnomah team for investing and believing in this message. Your ability to work the way you do is inspiring. Now being a part of the family, I see why you've had so much success. Thank you for letting me be a part it all.

To the Fedd Agency for working as hard as you do. Thank you, Esther, for showing me what hard work looks like and for fighting for me. I couldn't have done it without you. Whitney, you're brilliant. Your commitment to this project and to me is why the end result is what it is. Thank you. I'm honored to know you!

Diana Dennis, thank you for the countless writing sessions, phone calls, text messages, and e-mails. You stuck with me the entire way. I can't tell you how grateful I am to you.

Thank you to my previous PA, Narliebeth, and my current PA, Bria, for handling everything around this book and helping to keep my life together.

Hannah and Lindsay, thank you for every creative contribution you've made, from the website to the artwork. You're both brilliant.

Last, but most certainly not least, I want to thank my Christ Tabernacle family for your prayers and support. I love you all. Thank you for tirelessly serving and giving to reach our city for Jesus. Your growth and dedication to the Gospel is a constant encouragement to me

ABOUT THE AUTHOR

C hris Durso is the Senior Associate Pastor of Christ Tabernacle, a multicampus church with locations in Queens and Brooklyn, New York. He is the creative architect of the misfit movement. Before his new role, he was the youth and young adult pastor of Misfit NYC for over ten years, which is the next gen ministry of Christ Tabernacle. Chris resides with his wife, Yahris, and two children, Dylan and Chloe, in New York.